Thirty Nine
and
Letting Go

A Father's Journey Through a
Son's Addiction and Depression

John B. Jenkins

ISBN: 978-1-4834-6222-6 (sc)
ISBN: 978-1-4834-6221-9 (e)

Library of Congress Control Number: 2016919776

Because of the dynamic nature of the Internet, any web addresses or links contained in this book may have changed since publication and may no longer be valid. The views expressed in this work are solely those of the author and do not necessarily reflect the views of the publisher, and the publisher hereby disclaims any responsibility for them.

Any people depicted in stock imagery provided by Thinkstock are models, and such images are being used for illustrative purposes only.
Certain stock imagery © Thinkstock.

Lulu Publishing Services rev. date: 12/05/2016

CONTENTS

INTRODUCTION

This book is not a novel nor is it filled with "self-help" ideas. I offer no theories which may bring personal success or perhaps, world peace. This book is a story; it is my story and the story of my oldest son relating to his life and the journey we each have taken through it. It is a story of how a drug addicted and clinically depressed son, brother, and husband can find love and redemption in the arms of a Savior Who died for him way before my son was even thought of. It is a story of a villain; an evil master known as addiction, who seems to succeed in his destructive efforts but it is also a story of a deliverer, a loving God Who looks beyond fault to see need. This book is not filled with answers, but it is filled with experiences in which you may connect and find motivation to discover the answers you seek. I am not a doctor so I cannot give you exact diagnoses and I am not a counselor so I cannot provide much enlightenment. However, I am a father, and now I am a father who has lost a son to the consequences of addiction and depression and I can offer insight into a journey which I hope will help you in yours. Although your story will differ from mine and your circumstances not be the same, one thing remains sure and constant; God has not changed and He is the one hope we all have in common and can depend on. It is my prayer that you are blessed and encouraged by this book and discover comfort in knowing you are not alone in your journey.

CHAPTER 1

The End Before The Beginning

Yesterday I buried my oldest son.

Today, I begin writing this book. I am not sure how it will turn out but I hope the words on the pages will somehow help any prospective reader and in some way, give me much needed peace and closure.

When I say, "I buried my oldest son," I mean it in the most literal sense possible. My oldest son, Josh, died on June 17, 2016, and as a minister and pastor, I conducted his funeral service and made the arrangements for him to have full military rites at a veteran's cemetery near where we live in Dublin, Virginia. As a minister I have attended many grave side services in which the deceased veteran was provided military honors and without fail, the gun salute always catches me off guard with the loud explosions of the rifles and the sounds of the ejected empty shell casings clanging on the concrete. Yesterday was no different except this time the honor of the salute with the firing of the rifles and the clanging shells was being offered for my first born son. I am still numb and in a blurred state of unbelief when I try to come to terms with the events of the past two weeks.

Today, I also find myself a member of a club I never thought I would have to join or be connected with. In fact, all the members who belong to this club do so with great reluctance and regret and not one member is excited to be a part of it. No one wants to hold an office, serve on a committee and actually no elections are ever held. No meetings are ever scheduled and no business is ever discussed yet the onetime payment of dues is the most costly of any social or religious club I know. The club is known as "Parents Who Have Buried a Child" and it is the most unpopular social connection in every town and community across this great land and perhaps even throughout the world. There are no feelings of pride or prestige in being a member of this club, no one is jealous for being left out and I actually lose my breath when talking about it. I was forced to become a member of this club as a result of events beyond my control; or, at least that's what I want to believe. I am sure that a great number of my thoughts for the rest of my life will be focused on how I might have kept myself from being forced to become of member of such an unpopular and unrewarding club.

Two weeks ago on June 8, sometime around six or seven in the morning, Josh was involved in a single car crash on route 100 in Giles County, Virginia and after being examined by local rescue workers the decision was made to have him air lifted from the crash site directly to Carilion Roanoke Memorial Hospital in Roanoke, Virginia. He suffered a severe brain trauma in the accident and was unresponsive when examined by the doctors in the emergency department. We still do not know exactly what happened to cause the accident but based on his recent state of mind, it is likely that excessive drug use was involved. The impact to his head left him in a deep coma for several days with no signs of improvement in brain function and no response to the doctor's efforts to get some type of reflex action from him.

After eight days of watching him being kept alive by a ventilator and fed through a tube, his mother and I made the most dreaded decision a parent could ever be forced to make. Josh had made his wishes known many times and we knew he did not want to simply have an existence sustained by artificial means so we had him removed from the ventilator. With a fever sometimes reaching 105 degrees and erratic, struggling breaths, he survived thirty six hours before succumbing to his injuries and slipping into the arms of Jesus. Parents aren't supposed to watch their children die and then make the arrangements for them to be buried; it should be the other way around yet here we are and I wouldn't wish this pain on anyone. Losing a child creates an overwhelming emptiness and leaves an unexplainable void on the inside of a parent while at the same time; an invisible weight settles on your chest denying you any ease in breathing. It's so hard to explain and I hope you never know what I am talking about.

Millie and I were high school sweethearts. Her family had lost their home in 1972 as a result of the collapse of a slush pond dam in a coal mining community on Buffalo Creek, West Virginia. The event made national headlines and the tragedy left over 120 people dead and destroyed multiple communities as homes, schools, and businesses were all washed away. Sadly, the flood showed no favoritism as young and old alike fell victim to its destructive force from which babies were physically torn from the arms of their screaming mothers. Having stayed with a friend the night before the flood, Millie was separated from her family for a couple of days and was feared dead. Her family was actually informed of her supposed death and her father was asked to come to the local school where the deceased were being kept to identify her body. Of course, he didn't find her in the dozens of recovered bodies and word soon reached them that she was safe and sound at her friend's home. She often shares about the reunion she and her dad had when he finally made his way to her and she heard him call out her name.

After the flood, her family moved around for a few months and ended up in a country setting in Mercer County, West Virginia and she found herself enrolled at Matoaka High School where I also attended. We began to date and our relationship became more serious after I graduated in 1975 and she was to graduate the following year. Millie was from a family with strong faith in Christ, so most of our dating was at church and occasionally, we would go out on Saturday nights but only if I promised her mother I would be in church on Sunday. Having faithfully kept my promises, (Millie was and still is, worth it) it wasn't long until I made my personal journey down the center aisle of that little community church to confess Jesus Christ as my Lord and Savior. We were engaged shortly thereafter and married in March of 1976 while she was still in High School. She still gets a little miffed when she tells the story about how I had to write her an excuse for missing school on our wedding day! It is hard to believe that more than forty years have passed since we said our "I do's."

We were married for thirteen months when little Joshua Benson Jenkins came into our lives on April 11, 1977. Millie was past her due date and after an afternoon drive on a bumpy road, Josh began to wiggle his way toward daylight! Her water broke and she was admitted to the hospital and gave birth to our first born son less than twenty four hours later. I remember the nurses telling me I was too little to be a daddy and laughing at me when I tried to convince them I was Millie's husband and Josh's father. I had begun working in the coal mines just prior to our wedding and had been placed on midnight shift in the summer of 1976. I can still recall Millie awakening me in the middle of the day while I was sleeping to say to me; "Guess who's going to be a daddy?" We were just kids ourselves and now we were going to have to raise a child. Even though there were a million things which we had no clue we would face, I was not intimidated by the task before me and weighing a whopping 120 pounds, my scrawny, rib showing chest swelled with pride. I was going to be a daddy, WOW, no sweat, got this covered! So, both of us, just nineteen years old welcomed little Josh into our world and nothing has ever been the same since. I remember Millie's mom asking me if I thought I could ever love someone so much as I did my new son. Millie and I had been blessed with the most precious gift anyone could receive and now, we would do our best to raise him and teach him about life, Jesus and the things of the Kingdom of God. Josh was born on a Monday and the following Sunday he was presented to the Lord for dedication at our church only six days old.

I once heard it said; "You have to have a license to drive a car but any jerk can be a dad." I understood clearly what that meant, that all it takes to be a dad is to provide a seed but I wanted to be more, I wanted to be a real father. Millie and I were blessed with two sets of great parents and role models and I knew that to be the best earthly father I could be would require me to lay aside selfish ambitions and desires and dedicate myself to the task ahead. To some extent I feel like I succeeded in that quest, perhaps even as much or more as other fathers I know, but time would prove to me that I wasn't as strong or wise as I had hoped to be. I was not only a young father but a very young Christian as well yet I knew my best hope would be found in the instructions and examples given to me in the Holy Scriptures, the Bible. Therefore, with only a high school education and just a few months of spiritual experience, I purposed to become a student of God's Word. Gratefully, more than forty years later, I remain a student of His Word and though my faith may be tested from time to time, I am convinced of the love of God and unwavering in my belief in the immeasurable depths of His mercy and grace.

CHAPTER 2

Something Special About That Kid

At an early age it became clear to us that Josh had a unique understanding of the ministry of the Holy Spirit. He clearly understood the power of prayer and had the child-like faith we all wish we had. Hardly big enough to walk, he had contracted some type of stomach bug and had been very sick for two or three days. We were praying and believing for a touch from God but his condition remained unchanged. The family urged us to take him to the doctor or emergency room but by now it was the weekend and his pediatrician was out of the office so we decided to wait one more day. Millie stayed home from church with him on Sunday morning while I went on, but we decided to take him with us to the evening service. I was always first at church, unlocked the doors and made things ready for the service and was carrying Josh up the front steps with the church key in hand. He was limp as a wet dish cloth but when I opened the door and took one step inside, his little body straightened and he rolled out of my arms and before I could catch him, his tiny feet hit the floor running and off through the church he ran just like he always did. Fever was gone, stomach bug was gone and you wouldn't believe that just sixty seconds earlier he was so sick and unmoving. It was like he was saying; "Just get me to church and God will do the rest."

There was also the time that Josh, Millie and I were returning home from a visit with her parents. This was before car seats were mandatory and Josh was sort of standing in the back floor board while leaning between the two front seats. As we neared the intersection where a lady from our church lived, Josh said; "Poor Miss Turner, she hurt her leg." He seemed upset so Millie reassured him that Mrs. Turner was okay because we had seen her at church just a couple of days ago and she seemed fine. Nothing else was said about it but when we went to church on Sunday morning, the congregation was talking about how Sister Turner had fallen on Friday and broke a bone in her leg. The time? Right when Josh had made his statement! Folks often said there was something special about Josh.

Not only was Josh a sensitive child, he also demonstrated a gifted, artistic talent and at an early age and he would often have his mother draw Superman for him during church service and he would color in the spaces. I think he was about four years old when he told her that he no longer needed her assistance because by then, he could actually draw better than she could. Once Millie took him with her to a voting precinct and while she waited, Josh got down on his knees and used a chair as a table to draw. When it was time for her to vote, the lady next to her said she would keep an eye on him while Millie voted and she watched Josh draw his pictures. When Millie returned, the lady identified herself as a teacher and commented on the talent Josh had for art.

He was about five years old at that time and as he grew into a young man, art remained a passion of his and heaven only knows how many pictures he drew that would amaze most anyone but would be thrown away because they didn't meet his expectations of himself. He would spend hours alone in his room drawing and cleaning! He was so emphatic that his room be organized insomuch that we never had to tell him to clean it. Looking back now with the life education we have experienced, I can see signs of depression that back then were simply described as unique features.

Even though he weighed eight pounds, eleven ounces at birth, Josh was a small toddler and was underweight and undersized for most of his life. Before he reached the age of kindergarten, he developed a problem with his eyes which required surgery at Duke University Eye Center in Durham, North Carolina. Though it was successful, the surgery left him with a need for glasses which proved quite a burden for such a young, insecure boy. He weighed a whopping twenty seven pounds when he entered kindergarten and was always the smallest in his class. His high intelligence was never in question as he always had a keen insight into matters far above his maturity level and he learned at a rapid rate. Though certainly not Jesus, he reminded me of how Jesus must have appeared when he amazed the teachers of the law in the Jerusalem Temple when He was only age twelve.

In addition to his artistic and intellectual abilities, Josh also had a sneaky, devious side to him. He received his first kiss from a girl in kindergarten by telling her if she wanted to be his friend she would have to kiss him. Little Amy wanted to be his friend so she consented and laid one on him! Once in the first grade, Josh decided he didn't want to stay at school. We walked him to school because we lived in sight of it and I saw him go in the front door before I returned home. We had two neighbors who were the age of our parents and they loved Josh and later on Matt, our second son and did their best to spoil them. It seems that Josh had simply turned around, walked out of the school and instead of coming home he went to Mamaw Glenda's house next door. She called to let us know the moment before the school called to ask why he was absent. I never knew what spooked him that day but I am convinced it was a major issue to him.

There was also the time when he was still in first grade that he did something at school which resulted in him being scolded by his teacher. When his teacher asked him why he was behaving as he was, he told her he was upset because his dad told him he wasn't getting anything for Christmas because he had been bad. Well, you can imagine the amount of sympathy he received from not only his teacher but the other teachers she told. I remember well how coldly I was treated at the school Christmas programs and I had no clue as to why! It wasn't until late spring that someone finally let the cat out of the bag and I had a chance to tell his teacher it wasn't true. Josh had played her like a fiddle but left me hanging on a limb!

As he grew, Josh became more of what I call a "drama king." He would exaggerate details but would really amplify the negative of any situation. I am like that myself but not to the extreme measure Josh was. Again, as we look back, we recognize that some of his issues were signs of the depression which eventually would consume his life. So, imagine this, you are five years old, weigh less than thirty pounds, you wear glasses and you are one of, if the not the smartest kid in class. Unless things changed these issues spelled only one thing, a recipe for bullying which would come later. As young parents we couldn't afford the clothes and shoes which were popular at the time but we did the best we could. Josh noticed that a kid at school had the word "NIKE" spelled out on his shoes and he asked him what that meant. When told that the shoes were expensive and popular, Josh came home and proceeded to write the word on his shoes. He carefully outlined the letters and filled them in with ink only to later realize he had actually wrote the word "HIKE" instead of "NIKE". His insecurities always led him to overreact and overcompensate throughout his entire life.

I have to stop and go back for just a moment. Josh had prayed and prayed for a baby brother and on September 10, 1981, his prayers were answered as we welcomed Jonathan Matthew Jenkins into our little family. We have pictures of Josh showering Matt, as we call him, with love and kisses and it made all seem well with the world. However, there have never been two more opposite brothers since Jacob and Esau in the Bible. Josh was always the quiet; indoors type child and Matt….well, you always knew when Matt was around the house. With a love for sports and the outdoors, Matt and Josh shared little in common growing up in the same home. Just as Josh would most often have pen and paper in hand, Matt would most likely be found with ball and glove in his. Finding some measure of common ground soon became very difficult as each of them began to develop individual friendships and pursue their own interests.

Once, when they were very young and Matt was still sitting in a high chair for his meals, the sneaky side of Josh showed up in a comedic way. Both boys were eating Spaghettios for lunch and we had left them alone in the kitchen while we were doing something else in another part of the house. Josh came running in to tell us to come and see what Matt had done. When we arrived in the kitchen, there sat Matt with his face painted very artistically with spaghetti sauce. The sauce followed the contour of his face and it was immediately obvious that Matt had not done this to himself. Josh's fingerprints were clearly visible as he had convinced his younger brother to sit still long enough for him to complete his human art work!

Josh made it through his elementary school years without much difficulty but he was quick to catch on that being small, smart and having to wear glasses left you unpopular, unnoticed, and a target to be made fun of. He compensated with uncharacteristic behavior and intentional sub-par school work because he had determined he would fit in better if he was just a regular guy. While quiet as a mouse at home, it seems he was rowdy at school and wanted to be the center of attention which often resulted in disciplinary actions by administration. One great characteristic Josh possessed though was impossible for him to hide because he couldn't deny his sensitive nature. Josh always went with the underdog. If there was a kid who had any kind of disability or characteristic that left them a target for bullying or shunning, that was the kid Josh made friends with. He knew how it felt to be different and didn't want anyone else to feel like he did. This was a trait that he exhibited all thirty nine years of his life and one which made his mother and I very proud of him.

Unfortunately, as his depression and addiction gained more and more control in his life, Josh would often develop a "savior" mentality and felt like it was his responsibility to fix everyone else and solve their problems. It may be hard for others to understand but this complex he exhibited was very real to him and left him with guilt and self condemnation when he was unsuccessful in his efforts. His sensitivity gave him a love for abandoned and abused animals and he invested many hours and dollars caring for pets and neighborhood strays as well. He always took it hard when he lost a pet to illness or old age and did everything he possibly could to make their lives comfortable and pain free until they passed. I can't help but wonder if some type of Christian counseling for kids had been available when he was young, maybe Josh would have had a different journey through life. Actually, it may have been available but it would have been unthinkable to seek for it because depression and its symptoms were evil according to much of the church theology of the day.

The Southern West Virginia community we lived in offered only two types of schools for their k-12 educational programs. Elementary school consisted of grades k-6 and high school was grades 7-12. There were no middle schools, so Josh and his elementary school classmates suddenly found themselves in the seventh grade walking the same halls as high school seniors and every age in-between. I am not exaggerating in the least when I say Josh found himself surrounded by boys more than two and three times his size. He was concerned that he would be picked on and his fears were quickly realized. Not violently, or even so much physically, but verbally as he was made fun of for his size and his glasses. I remember when he came home one day with a smile on his face because he had made a new friend. He told his mom he didn't have to worry anymore because his new friend, Will, was as big as the seniors. Will and Josh remained friends and after graduation Will married Josh's first cousin Christy. Of course Will was also a seventh grader and had to work his own way through school days with older boys and girls but he was always a source of encouragement and friendship for Josh.

Josh's size and lack of interest kept him out of the sports arena. His talents were clearly creative in nature and he never understood the fascination people had with sports and being an athlete. Although he did try baseball one season, mainly because of peer pressure and a desire to fit in, he didn't find his niche until he enrolled in a karate class. He was a natural and each time he was tested for belt advancement he did so with ease and caught the attention of other instructors. One such instructor literally begged us to allow her to train Josh but logistics were difficult and I decided it would be too inconvenient. Looking back I really wish I hadn't been so close minded but I was yet to realize how much karate meant to him. He did accomplish a black belt ranking very quickly and karate always held a special place in his heart. Josh developed a measure of self esteem from such accomplishments and it grieved him when later surgeries and his physical condition would deny him the opportunity to rediscover his love for karate.

By now, Josh's creativity in art was very apparent and he would spend hours in his room or sitting on the couch just drawing. Sometimes he would draw something he had seen but mostly he drew what was in his mind. He would sketch out pictures of Jesus and Mary, superheroes and villains, and everything in between. Every line and shadow had to be perfect or he would either start over or just throw it away. He was not very interested in television for reasons he never shared but I think he was probably more entertained by his own thoughts.

Those were the days when people thought the word "depression" was a cop-out or just an excuse for unusual behavior. I have to admit, the thought of Josh battling depression never entered our minds. We had even heard teaching that depression was only from the devil and to consider such a thing was a sign of unbelief or even blasphemy. We listened to people who said there was no possible way that depression could be a real disease and all a person needed to do was rebuke the devil and decide to be happy. Sadly, I must admit there have been times, early in my ministry, that I made the same or similar uneducated assumptions but Josh's life has been an education for me and our entire family. Hopefully, I will never again be that inconsiderate of the struggles that we now know so many others also face. Taking this journey with my son has caused me to acknowledge that mental illness is a real medical issue and manifests itself in many ways including clinical depression.

Before continuing I feel compelled to say this; when I imply that Josh presented sub-par school work in his classes, I mean sub-par to his capabilities. He still graduated with honors and was awarded a scholarship to a college not far from our home. I will mention more about that later.

CHAPTER 3

Two-Sided Coin

Please don't think this book is simply a biography of Josh's life. I am trying to show you that we were just an ordinary American family and Josh grew up in a simple, stable and Christian environment. We worked our jobs, paid our bills, went to church, made time for our children and still, depression and addiction found him and led him to an early grave. And please understand this; I am not blaming symptoms or diseases for his problems nor am I casting stones at any of his friends because at the end of the day, we are all products of the decisions we make. We are responsible and failure to realize that makes recovery almost impossible. However, I just ask that people try to understand that we are all subjected to different types of influences and temptations and some of them are more difficult than others to rise above and conquer. If just one family or one individual can see themselves in these words and make adjustments in their lives to avoid what our son suffered, then to me it will be worth the effort to write this book. I do not want to see anyone go through what Josh and those of us who loved him endured during his struggle.

Even though school was a place where Josh always felt engaged in an uphill battle, there was a place where he was respected and admired regardless of his size and physical limitations. Since her childhood, Millie was raised in church and she loved it and after I made the decision to follow Christ and Josh came along, church became the single most important item of our lives. As we grew in our faith and our relationship with Christ, we found ourselves in a denomination which offered friendly competitions for young people to test their Bible knowledge and to demonstrate artistic ability. Josh had finally hit the jackpot! The Bible Quiz contests were age appropriate and Josh never lost in individual competitions. As he grew older, he competed with teams which won most of the time with him frequently being awarded high scorer honors. I have to insert a plug here for our other son Matt, who was equally successful in Bible Quiz competitions but also received honors in national events having been awarded a trophy for National High Scorer one year.

Thinking back on those days I am reminded of one particular event in which Josh buzzed in early to answer a question. The quizmaster had only uttered a couple of words of the question when Josh hit his buzzer. The rules required that a pre-mature response required the competitor to not only answer correctly, but to also finish the question! No one seemed to know what to do next since clearly a default had occurred but Josh spoke up and said he would finish the question before answering. With jaws dropped open, we sat there as he did just that then answered the question correctly. He took his Bible Quizzing very seriously!

Such competitions in a friendly, non-judgmental environment, allowed Josh to fully express his abilities with confidence and he did so also with his art. He received much praise and several awards for some of the amazing things he drew but was most proud of his ability in the Bible competitions. I guess when you consider church and school in the same sentence, his life was somewhat like a two-sided coin. I have to admit though; it was sort of comical to watch the reactions of members from other teams when Josh showed up. All of them much bigger in size than he was, probably with more friends than he had, would lower their heads in disappointment when this scrawny little kid made his appearance and each of them would have loved to be his friend and teammate.

I have learned a few things in my forty plus years in the church and I am not just referring to verses from the Bible. I have also been a school bus driver for several years and believe me, we drivers see the kids in ways parents and churches never do. Life is difficult for young people today with the decline in moral expectations and pressures to try new things. Although we all want to believe the kid we see sitting on the church pew on Sunday morning is the same as the one we send out into the world each day, it just isn't so. There are a lot of two-sided coins in this world and too many parents are blinded by just focusing on the side they want to see.

No parent wants to think their child will ever have addictive issues, severe depression with suicidal thoughts and tendencies but refusing to consider it only eases their conscience and denies the possibility of a reality they are afraid to face. I was, I am, that parent.

But, maybe we shouldn't be so surprised when it happens because today's music, video games and social media is filled with sex, violence and hatred and it greatly influences how young people view themselves and the people and things in their lives. For whatever reason, many young people today are simply uncaring and unmoved by the sadness and tragedy happening all around them.

Millie and I raised our kids in church, they went to Sunday school and attended Vacation Bible School summer after summer so surely we have earned points with the Almighty and He will spare them such troubles. Sounds right doesn't it? Isn't that what we sometimes think? That grace can be earned by good works? Don't we sometimes scratch our head when it seems like bad things happen to good people? Since sin entered the world all those thousands of years ago; no one, and I do mean no one, has escaped the destructiveness sin has produced. Some more, or perhaps less than others, but all have suffered from its clutches in one way or another. Oh, I know your theology may deny that but look around, look beyond the walls of your church or your own box and see the truth. Many things we Christians profess we believe never come to reality in our lives and we are told we lack faith if we admit it. This journey with my son has helped me accept that I can be a realist and still be a person of faith.

I ask you to consider that people are hurting all around you today and some of them may be dear to your heart and you don't even know it yet. I urge you to not ignore the signs and bury your head in the sand while hoping it all disappears. Let's give some glory to God though! Thanks to the gift of eternal life through Jesus Christ our Lord, we have the hope, the expected assurance of a place and a life free from all the struggles this life offers! And while we are still here, we have the promise that He never leaves or forsakes us but goes with us till the end. Wow, what a Savior we serve!

CHAPTER 4

Now What?

In June of 1995, the first graduating class of Pikeview High School (which was the result of consolidating four smaller schools) was thrust out into what we parents always called; "the real world." The most frequently asked question had to be; "now what?" Can you remember how you felt when your tassel was turned and you launched your cap into the air? Maybe your plans were already made and in process, or perhaps you were just going to wing it and see what developed. Josh was no different. He was like the hundreds of thousands across America who were graduating that spring and time was not going to pause for any of them. The real world would be a rude awakening as high school graduates would now become the little fish in a much bigger pond!

That awakening hit Josh right between the eyes when applying for a job. He had asked us over and over to allow him to get an ear ring but Millie told him he would have to wait until he was eighteen years old. His eighteenth birthday came and off to the mall he went to get his ear pierced and sure enough, he did it. About a week passed before he went to a job interview and the man told him that regardless of how qualified Josh was, he would not hire any man with a ring in his ear. Just as quickly as it went in, the ear ring came back out and stayed out, much to the delight of his mother.

I would like to tell you that as a teenager Josh never drank, never partied, never smoked pot and never worried us but I would also like to tell you the same about myself, but I can't. Well, I could but I would be lying. Peer pressure is a true enemy to young people when considering their faith. All of the "thou shall not's" suddenly butting heads with the new "why not's" can leave a young Christian confused and the guilt and condemnation that religious legalism presents doesn't help either. So, I know for a fact, there was some behavior exhibited that was sufficient to make a worried dad sit up at night to watch for the headlights of a car showing me he was safely home. I can think of some times that I probably should have confronted or at least questioned him, but I settled for being thankful he was safely home and hopefully it wouldn't happen again. I later realized that my passive behavior was also a problem and I was becoming an enabler even though I had never heard the word at that time.

When I look back over the forty years that Millie and I have been married, (thirty nine with kids), I can't recall one certain decision or event that would identify me as an enabler, but I know now that somewhere along the line it happened. Sometimes a misguided desire to help can easily become an act of enablement and an opportunity for growth is lost in a simple gesture of kindness. I was working youth camp several years ago and my responsibility was handling the safety line for young kids trying to ascend a climbing wall. There was one kid from my church and he couldn't make it up the wall very far so I gathered a couple more volunteers and together we pulled him up just so he could at least say he made it to the top. I can still hear the voice of the camp director as he looked at me and said; "I am going to start calling you Pastor Enabler." What I thought was helping was actually denying a young person the responsibility to learn on their own and either succeed or fail based on their own efforts.

We live in a world that now rewards both success and failure as we see all young competitors in sporting competitions receive a trophy or ribbon. Political correctness now demands we honor equally and in doing so, we deny young people the privilege from learning from their own mistakes and failures. I have come to understand that many of the decisions I made in Josh's life to always "fix" his problems instead of helping him learn how to fix them, were poor decisions resulting in unfortunate outcomes. Failure and loss are as much a part of life as success and reward and are essential elements of the learning process so we must allow them to challenge and motivate us instead of defeat and discourage us.

Josh always kept some type of job which kept him active but mostly kept him out of the house and out of church. He spent a lot of nights with friends either before or after work and there were many times I should have insisted on him staying home. I was passive with him and just hoped he was doing the right things but hindsight proves it was just wishful thinking. As I mentioned earlier, he had received a scholarship to attend a local college and enrolled to begin classes during the fall after his graduation and although he seemed like a fish out of water, he made it through one year receiving credits for all his classes. It was a difficult year for me as a parent though because he communicated with us less than normal which wasn't much to begin with. Josh spent too much time living in his own head and what we concluded to be normal teenage behavior, was actually indications of his undisclosed depression.

His selection of friends left us concerned but I have always been careful not to call other peoples kids "the wrong crowd" because that's just passing blame for our own kid's failures. None of his behavior patterns seemed much different than thousands of other boys his age and we figured millions of other parents were facing the same things, and they were. However, Josh seemed to be over-compensating in some areas to fit in with his circle of influence, or at least it seemed that way to me. I remember one time in which two friends came home with him from school because they were all getting ready for a class trip. However, before we arrived home from work, Josh and his two friends decided to go see a female classmate who lived just down the road from us. I still don't know why, but they thought it would be a good idea to take some eggs from our fridge and throw them at her house. Of course, she told on them and I made them all go with bucket and brush in hand to clean the raw egg off the side of the house. Naturally, the parents of the other two boys never found out but I reacted in anger and wouldn't allow Josh to go on the trip as his punishment. I don't think he ever forgot or forgave me for that and it could be one reason we were never as close as we should have been. Even though he occasionally attended, he had little or no interest in church so his mother and I just waited for him to snap out of it and recognize his potential. We prayed for him and asked God to send him the right girl to complete his life. God was already on the job!!

During his high school years Josh had become close friends with Melissa Dawn Midkiff who lived not far from where we did. Actually, Millie and I went to school with her parents so our families already had some connections. Josh and Melissa became each other's listening partner as they shared their troubles and life problems. Josh would give her a ride to school and back and I can remember Millie telling him that neither he nor Melissa would ever find somebody if they spent all their time together! Well, they hadn't realized it yet but God had already decided they were to be more than friends and they eventually got the message. During Josh's freshman year at college he and Melissa grew closer and eventually a more serious relationship began.

Against our hopes and wishes, Josh decided not to return to college for his sophomore year and thought he would just work a job until he could figure out what he really wanted to do with his life. There was a pattern of behavior in my life that was now becoming readily apparent to Millie and others who knew us well. I am referring to my actions as an enabler. You see, when my kids became old enough to drive and wanted a car so they could take themselves to school and/or work, I helped them buy one. Not a big deal you may say, countless others have done the same. Yes, perhaps, but I would buy a new or newer car and let them have it, then I would take the older car for myself. I told myself I did this because I wanted them to have dependable transportation but really I just didn't want their friends to see them driving what I ended up driving. There were times when they were unable to make the payments on the newer car and I would bail them out.

Eventually, Josh came to realize that no matter what problem he faced, dad would always find a way to remedy the situation. It was a pattern of behavior which exhibited itself until the end of his life. Not daily, mind you, but often enough to allow a relationship of father and son develop in an unhealthy manner. Please do not think it is my intention to make Josh sound like a bad son because he wasn't. In fact, I imagine there are many fathers and sons with similar relationships and stories that had a happier ending than ours and I hope they are able to appreciate what they have. I am just trying to share the elements of our lives which I feel may have possibly contributed to the outcome of his life. Believe me, for every sad story I may share, there were dozens in which we laughed, loved and enjoyed the great mysteries of the lives God had blessed us with.

Josh seemed like a lost puppy the summer and fall after his freshman year but he had been tossing around the idea of joining the military. My older brother, Barry, had spent twenty three years in the Air Force and retired as a Captain having enjoyed a very successful military career. My career choices had been much less appealing so Josh had developed a keen interest in talking with his uncle about life in the Air Force. It seemed to be a way for him to get a new start with other candidates on a level playing field so he began leaning in that direction more and more. I remember the day he came home and out of nowhere told me he had decided to "Aim High." You may remember that as being the Air Force recruiting slogan. However, he had a "but" to add to it. He said that first, he and Melissa were going to be married. My greatest concern of him joining the military and leaving home was being alone. He had been so prone to give in to peer pressure in the past but with someone to come home to each day, I felt he could conquer his personal insecurities. We were delighted with his decision(s) and loved Melissa as our own daughter from the beginning.

Josh and Melissa both worked jobs during the fall and winter of 1996-1997 and a wedding date had been set for April, 1997. Josh was scheduled to leave for basic training the following June so after the wedding, they both lived with us and they also spent time at Melissa's moms house as well. As they headed out of town for their honeymoon after the wedding reception, they did so in our best automobile. I was worried that Josh's car may not be the best option so they took Millie's. I remember they made it as far as Charlotte, North Carolina on that Saturday evening with their ultimate destination as Daytona Beach, Florida. Millie worked as a legal secretary at that time and her boss owned a condo right on the beach. He would give his employees a free week's stay each year if they wanted it and he was gracious enough to let Josh and Melissa have our week for that year.

Late Sunday afternoon Josh called to say all the brake lights had come on in our car and he was scared to drive it. I told him not to panic but just plan to stay one more night in Charlotte and we would see what we could do on Monday morning. Having been a former car salesman, I located the nearest Pontiac Dealership which happened to be about two blocks away from the motel where they were staying. I called the dealership early Monday morning, explained the situation and they said it would be safe for Josh to bring the car to them. He did just that and they quickly found the problem and fixed it. Millie's car had just crossed over the limit of mileage for the warranty but they took care of it free of charge anyway.

We were very grateful and the two newlyweds were on their way to Florida that afternoon. Looking back, I should have advised him what to do but instead I did it all for him having taught him nothing but instead, simply increased his dependency on me.

As I look back over our lives I can see there are many things I wish I could have a "do-over" for. I was never a hunter or a fisherman but I should have encouraged my sons to experience those things for themselves. I never learned the basic things of auto repair but I should have made sure they knew what to do when it became necessary. I was a fair carpenter but I was so impatient when my boys were young, I never took the time to teach them what I knew. What they have learned they have done so on their own without the help of a teaching father. I realize now what I should have done and I should not have been surprised when Josh became so dependent on me to fix things for him.

CHAPTER 5

Out With the Old, In With the New

After the honeymoon was over, the countdown began for the day Josh would leave for basic training in San Antonio, Texas. I don't know who dreaded it most, Josh, Melissa, Millie or me! Well, actually I do know, it was Josh. I was dreading seeing my son who was just a few inches taller than five feet, weighing maybe 120 pounds ringing wet and still wearing those glasses which kept one weak eye in line with the other, enter the world of the United States Air Force where boys are either made into men or just weaker boys. Josh simply dreaded leaving Melissa. She had become his life very quickly and he worried about her well-being all the time she was out of his sight. He just couldn't imagine being apart from her for six weeks. It consumed his every thought. He wasn't concerned about the Texas heat, the long days of Basic Training, the threatening voice of the drill instructor, just Melissa. Josh never could handle loss very well and the thought of her safety and care not being in his immediate control and oversight terrified him. However, he put his head down and plowed through it all determined to be successful for both their sakes. They had survived their teenage years, solidified their self esteem with marriage and now the foundation for a promising future was before them. Actually, it was an exciting time even though emotions naturally ran high.

Just as all the final preparations for his departure were climaxing, a hiccup arrived. Josh was diagnosed with a small heart murmur as a child but we were told he would grow out of it. But now, at age twenty, the doctor said it was still there. Our first thoughts were; "Is this serious enough to prevent him from joining the Air Force?" Josh, who already operated on a very negative side of any situation, became convinced that everything they had hoped for was now lost. So, off to the doctor we went, that's right, Josh, Melissa and me. I was going to make sure all the right questions were asked and all the right answers were given and that is exactly what I did. In the end it was no big deal and had no effect on Josh entering the military. Once again, dad had come to the forefront to face the mountain his son had to face and once again dad led in conquering the mountain. Good parenting? Maybe….but more like being an enabler. If I could fix a problem or at least attempt to do so, I found it easier than letting him try on his own. Besides, he would be gone soon and I would never have a chance to fix a problem again…..or so I thought.

Before we knew it the day had arrived for his departure for basic training. It was out with the old and time to bring in the new. For sure, this was a life changing moment in both of their lives and if everything went well, Josh and Melissa would never be the same. The opportunities and experiences awaiting them could surely grow and mature them both into capable and independent people who could conquer anything and be successful on their own. But watching him get out of the car and walk away to enter this brave new world by himself for at least six weeks, was the hardest thing that Melissa, Millie and I had ever done up to that point. I can't imagine what was going through his mind as he looked back to wave that one last time before disappearing from our sight. I know his heart was breaking and his emotions were telling him to turn around but we are so proud that he kept going and boarded that airplane to a new life. However, all of our hopes and pride in his decision weren't quite enough to keep back the tears flowing from the sadness of seeing him go. Our oldest son had grown up and was well on his way to becoming a proud member of the United States Air Force. It was one of the greatest decisions he ever made and to look back now at his accomplishments while in the Air Force still makes us all very proud of him.

His recruiter had told him he would be allowed to make one short call home his first weekend in basic training. The call would be ten minutes and the intended purpose would be to give his family basic information such as his address where he could receive mail. I was so afraid he would be emotional when he called that I had prayed for God to make a way that I would not be the one to answer the phone since there was no caller

ID at the time. Melissa worked in housekeeping at a motel about twenty five minutes from our home and she had not yet started driving. Josh, her mom, or Millie and I had always taken her where she needed to go so it wasn't a big deal. He knew what time she was supposed to get off work and be back at our house so he timed his call until then. However, Melissa had injured herself that particular day and had to be checked out at the local emergency room and I had limited details of what had happened. Millie had gone to pick her up, Matt was outside shooting basketball and I was alone in the house when the phone rang.

Josh was an emotional wreck as he began the conversation with telling me to quickly write down his address. As I did so, I could hear his drill instructor in the background screaming at him while counting down the seconds remaining for his call. Just as soon as I had the address information, he asked to speak to Melissa and couldn't understand why she wasn't home yet. As he pushed for information, the instructor screaming the countdown in the background, I told him she had hurt herself and had to stop by the emergency room just to be checked out. He didn't take the news well and as I was trying to reassure him that it was just a minor incident, his time ran out and the Instructor ended his call. At that precise moment, Millie and Melissa pulled into the drive-way. I stood speechless as I had failed to comfort my son and now was unable to comfort my daughter-in-law who was crying due to missing his call. She, of course, was fine medically but he would have to wait until a letter arrived from her to get the details he needed to calm down. He later said it was a tough few days before that letter arrived but instead of focusing on how it might benefit him from having to learn how to trust, I just felt guilty like I had failed him and Melissa because I couldn't fix their pain.

These were the days before the world wide web and emails were unheard of as yet. No additional phone calls were allowed so all the communication we had were the letters we all exchanged. Of course by the time we received a letter we realized that whatever mood he was in when he wrote it had long since passed and we had no idea how he was actually doing at the time. The year he had spent at college granted him the honor of entering basic training with his first step in rank already awarded to him. Though I'm sure he had his tough moments, Josh put his head down and plowed his way through "boot camp" as it is called, and graduation day was fast approaching. Millie, Melissa, Matt and I packed the car and headed to San Antonio to share in his accomplishment. We were allowed to spend a little time with him before and after graduation and though it was clear he missed Melissa, he was determined to continue on to the next step which was technical school in Wichita Falls, Texas. His last words to us before we left San Antonio was to tell us he would be permitted to find a place off base after a couple of weeks in Wichita Falls and at that time we would be able to bring Melissa back out to him to stay.

He was exactly right and almost two weeks to the day we were packed up and headed back out to Texas. This time Matt stayed home with some friends from church and this gave us some room for most of Melissa's personal things. We arrived at Wichita Falls and helped to get them settled into a tiny little apartment just off base. Josh had bought a bicycle which he used as transportation and it seemed to work pretty well. He rode the bike on and off base to his classes and was able to ride it to a little grocery store nearby to pick up what they needed. When they left Wichita Falls he simple leaned the bicycle up against the wall of the apartment complex and figured someone else could benefit from it. Although they had few amenities, both were very happy because they were together at last and the road before them had just become a lot easier to travel. They had no idea where they would go next but as long as they were together, they would be happy and so would we! It seemed like the difficult past was behind them and the sky would be the limit for the future awaiting them.

At this time it is worth noting that Josh was successful at every level in the Air Force. He had been commended in basic training as well as technical school. To this day, I still cannot fully grasp the difficulty he lived with as he could be an emotional wreck one minute and a fully focused Airman the next. Though his emotions could propel him into depression, he was still able to rise above it and achieve success at whatever he set out to do. He would battle with negativity but seemed to always have the strength and courage to work hard and excel at every level. I think that most of us are that way to some extent. We all have our insecurities and emotional battles but somehow find a way to put them aside long enough to do what it takes to make it in this world. However, with Josh it just seemed like there was a greater distance between his high and low points than it was with most other people. This proved to be the case when in his worst years; he was diagnosed with bi-polar disorder which explained why he operated at two totally opposite spectrums of his mental and emotional abilities. These are not excuses for later behavior but simply conditions which helped him and us to learn how to compensate for his up and down life moments.

As I have already said, the things our family experienced with Josh have been an education and many of my friends would disagree with my conclusions and I respect their right to do so. But, there are many more who have seen what we have seen and not only agree with me, but also have experienced the same. People have a tendency to measure everyone else's problems by their own. All illnesses are not the same and do not affect everyone the same. For example, I have suffered from migraine headaches since I was a teenager and have had every test possible to determine the cause but to no avail. It was only when I began to take a certain blood pressure medicine that the headaches stopped. The doctors do not know what connection the medicine has to the headaches but as long as I need the medicine, they will leave me on it and I will receive double benefit from it.

I have heard people say things like they have worked all day with a migraine and I would disagree wholeheartedly! They may have worked with a bad headache but not a legitimate migraine. I have lain on the floor with my head against the cool toilet bowl trying to find relief, I have beaten my head against the wall to try to change the pain and I have literally prayed to die! I did not even want someone to speak to me because forming a thought in my mind increased the pain in my head. Those who have been diagnosed with migraine headaches know what I am talking about. I have heard people say that they have been depressed but prayed their way out of it so everyone else should be able to do the same. Shame on us for having such narrow-minded responses which only come across as insensitivity to those suffering from clinical depression. We all have moments and even days where we may be depressed but that is a far cry from someone who suffers deep depression every moment of every day. Just as a bad headache is not automatically a migraine, neither is a season of being depressed the same as clinical depression. Josh could have won millions of dollars in the lottery but his depression would not have changed because it was more than a temporary condition, for him it was a mental illness.

CHAPTER 6

Where?

With Melissa with him in Wichita Falls, Josh was able to concentrate on his technical education and prepare himself for his next assignment. He was told his next base could be anywhere in the world and in some assignments; he may not be able to bring Melissa with him. Back we go to square one! Josh became convinced he would be shipped over-seas somewhere unheard of and Melissa would have to come back home for a year or maybe even two. Naturally, we all panicked a bit because there was nothing we could do to affect his next assignment and the requirements which accompanied it.

We understood that if the Air Force wanted him in some remote part of the world then it was their right to send him there. He had taken an oath to serve anywhere they assigned him and if that was the case, he would have to learn how to get by on his own for an extended period of time. Easier said than done! Well, the day finally came when his first base assignment was to be disclosed to him and sure enough, it was a remote assignment, in a far away place known as North Dakota! "Where,... North Dakota?" It seemed that the Air Force Base in Grand Forks, North Dakota, was considered a remote assignment and it was possible that he would be there for the remainder of his four year enlistment. "Whew.... Jesus on the mainline, tell Him what you want!"

We were all thankful and excited that they would be stationed here on the mainland of the United States and just be a short flight away or a two day drive. Josh had told me that he would need to buy a car just as soon as they got home from technical school and they would have a few days to get ready before leaving for Grand Forks. Instead of waiting for them, I went to a car dealership, picked out the car I thought they could afford, made the financing arrangements and sealed the deal. All they had to do was drive it away. Sadly, Josh never learned the art of negotiating a car deal and was taken advantage of multiple times in his life when dad wasn't with him. They were happy with the little Chevrolet Cavalier and had it packed completely full of their stuff when they finally headed out on their own to North Dakota.

My son had many talents and abilities in which he excelled, but driving a car was not among them! He simply always seemed preoccupied with other thoughts when driving and I admit I was greatly concerned with him behind the wheel of a car all the way to Grand Forks, North Dakota. I was so relieved when he called on that Friday afternoon to tell us they had arrived and was already in the housing unit provided for them. They used a microwave box for a table, an air mattress for a bed and another box for a lamp table but they were together and they were happy. God is good! Prior to heading across country, we found out that part of the base housing in Grand Forks had suffered some damage the previous year due to unexpected flooding of the Red River and it was a possibility there would be no place for them to stay. However, Josh was not going to leave Melissa home and the Lord was very gracious in making sure housing was indeed available when they arrived.

It didn't take long for the Air Force to ship what little bit of furniture they had accumulated and with nothing but a small car payment, they were able to buy all the things needed to furnish their first home together. Josh quickly settled into his new job at the small medical clinic on base and Melissa found a job at a little pizza restaurant just outside the front gate. They were young but they were plenty capable of making it on their own and Josh soon taught Melissa how to drive and things were progressing nicely. They made new friends and developed their own social circle and just one more thing was needed....a church. I think they visited a couple of places but found a little church not far from the base and both of them loved it and the congregation. It was nothing fancy, just a simple church with a mission to share the love of Christ with whomever they could. The Pastor and his family quickly befriended the both of them providing some much needed stability and focus in their lives.

Josh was a self taught drummer and loved all types of music. Melissa has a beautiful voice and both joined the praise team at the church. However, one thing was lacking, the church didn't have a set of drums for Josh to play. Millie and I were charter members of New Vision Church in Princeton, West Virginia, and it was also the church Josh had attended with us before leaving for the Air Force. Additionally, he and Melissa had been married there. When I mentioned the situation to the church it took about two seconds for them to decide to buy the drum set and ship it directly to the church in North Dakota. It was just a matter of a few days before the little church in Grand Forks had a new set of drums and their own drummer to play them. It was in that little church that Josh matured spiritually and developed a greater sense of responsibility that would be reflected in later accomplishments. The Pastor mentored Josh and was like a father figure to him and we were happy and proud of how they were doing. On a side note, Millie, Matt and I made three different trips to visit them during our spring breaks and were blessed to worship with them on Easter Sunday.

It was the fall of 1997 when Josh and Melissa arrived in Grand Forks to begin their new military life and we were all very proud of them and the courage they had shown. Back home Millie was working as a Legal Secretary, I was the Director of a local Credit Counseling Agency and Matt was in high school. We were very active in the church and faithful in attendance, church work and tithing. Our Pastor used to say we were the best of members because we gave much and needed little. Our life was the church and still is, not the building but Christ and His mission. God had been so good to us and we always just wanted to be a part of something that promoted His message and gave glory to Him. We raised our kids in church teaching them Biblical values and did our best to demonstrate them at home and in community. We have never considered our service to God as confining and restricted but instead, serving Him has given us the freedom to truly enjoy life. However, some have considered our faith commitments to be excessive and we have often been rejected and criticized for it but that's a small price to pay for what Jesus did for us.

I think Millie was born a Christian! At least if that is possible, because from a child she has always loved the Lord. She tells stories of how she used to sing in church while standing on a box behind the pulpit so people could see her. Of course I won't mention the fact that members of the congregation used to give her a quarter to sing! She still loves to sing and to this day does so as often as she has the opportunity, especially when we are out ministering somewhere together. She was raised in a Christian home and has often spoken of the times that she and her dad would go to church on Sunday night and she loved it because it was their time together. He was the biggest source of encouragement for Millie and myself when we ventured out into ministry later on, especially for me personally.

Although not perfect, Millie grew up with strong Christian values and is still the most conservative person I know! It was our desire that our children grow up to appreciate the same values we did but I think maybe, we tried too hard. I really believe that there were times my family would have benefited from spending quality time together doing something we all enjoyed instead of insisting we be in church every time the doors were opened. I know that most Pastor's wouldn't say that but sometimes we need to remember that the unit of family should come first. As I look back on our lives I feel great regret for not taking advantage of opportunities to invest more time in my sons when I had the chance.

My story is a bit different. Although raised by two wonderful and loving parents, I was not raised in church. My grandfather was a minister and he lived with us but church attendance wasn't a big item in our home. My mom and dad were great parents and good, honest people but attending church was just not something we did as a family. My sister Sherry attended church with her friends and I would sometimes go here or there, mostly because of some girl, but I never made any type of commitment. However, there was always a tug in my heart that I later understood to be conviction and perhaps a calling, and I felt like my journey would someday include a real relationship with Christ. I remember how as a kid I would argue the Bible with other kids but none of us knew what we were talking about. We would base our beliefs on what we wanted to be true so naturally we had no proof to back it up. Sounds a little bit like what still goes on in church today!

On our very first date before we got a half mile from her grandmother's house, Millie looked at me and said; "I need to tell you that you will never be anymore than second place in my life." Wow! What a thing to say to a guy on a first date! She was telling me that God would always be first and I have to admit that right then and there, I was a little bit jealous of God! Normally, something like that would be fighting words but I wasn't quite ready to challenge the Creator of the Universe to a fist fight. I grew to understand what she meant and as I said before, her mom insisted I attend church with them while we were dating so it wasn't long until I made my own decision to follow Christ and I can honestly say I have never looked back since. There is a funny thing I will share concerning Millie's mom. Her name was Gracie and since she made me attend church I used to tell people that now I understand what Paul meant when he wrote to the Ephesian church that "By Grace are ye Saved." Her mom used to get a big kick out of that even though she would never admit it.

In March of 1983, I acknowledged an internal leading into the ministry. It was a calling that led us away from the church we attended and dearly loved and landed us in a different denomination with people we didn't really know. However, God knew what He was doing and I began preaching. I was awful! The first step in recovery is admitting the problem and I was awful! I was preaching what I heard others preach and so it had no freshness of revelation. I quickly learned to study on my own and pray for God to help me and I finally got a little better. I am still surprised today when someone invites me back the second time!

Millie's family had some talent when it came to singing so we put together a gospel group and traveled from church to church singing and sometimes we would be invited to preach as well. Josh, Matt along with nieces and nephews traveled with us but they weren't quite as excited about the process as we were. They would quickly grow bored with the same thing over and over and I guess we should have paid better attention because they were quickly losing interest in church altogether. As parents and adults we sometimes assume our children are okay with the Lord because we take them to church again and again. However, we often times fail in making sure those same children actually have a personal relationship with Jesus and are not just going through religious motions. After a few years of the gospel music ministry, Millie and I committed ourselves to the new ministry of New Vision church and stayed there seventeen years.

So, the stage is set; Millie and I are settled at New Vision, Matt is finishing high school and preparing for college, Josh and Melissa are content for the moment in North Dakota and everything seems great. We communicate with them two or three times a week by phone and so we enter into a time of peace, or, so we thought.

CHAPTER 7

A Time of Testing

We were just a run of the mill, down to earth, Christian and American family who worked their jobs, paid their bills and made contributions to church and society just like millions of others across this land. We loved our country and paid our taxes but still, there was nothing special about us, our kids or anyone in our family. Millie and I loved God, our kids, our families and each other. We combined our incomes, shared responsibilities at home and did practically everything together. The only time we were ever apart was when we were working so it shouldn't have been a surprise when the enemy of our souls attacked us at the places we worked. It wasn't our faith he zeroed in on, it wasn't our finances, it wasn't even our health. He attacked our marriage. I mean he literally came at us with both barrels blazing spreading lies and making accusations. No wonder the scriptures identify him as the accuser of the brethren and the father of lies. I was the one being lied on and accused of things I would never have done or said and I didn't even know what was going on until we reached a pressure point in our relationship. But, God is faithful, and at just the right moment He exposed the lies and accusations as being false and Millie and I emerged from the trial more in love than ever and determined to hold fast to our faith and each other. I guess it is true that what doesn't kill you makes you stronger!

Troubles drive you to your knees when you look to God for guidance and I sure spent a lot of time praying during our struggle. You see, I was oblivious to what the enemy was doing so it was difficult to know exactly how to pray. At that time my place of employment was actually less than a mile from where we attended church so I spent my lunch period at our church altar praying. I cried, I pleaded, I made deals with God along with promises to do things differently if He would just fix this. You know what I'm talking about; I imagine we all have prayed like that at times. When I finally got serious with God and laid it all out on the altar, He finally spoke and as usual He didn't say what I wanted to hear.

God showed me that instead of trying to get Him to fix others, I needed to look deep into self and see if I had truly loved and honored my wife as He had instructed me in the scriptures. I didn't like what I saw and I immediately made a commitment to begin to love and honor her as God's greatest, earthly gift to me. That allowed me to pray for her in ways I never had before. That's why the victory we enjoyed means so much to us because we had to take part in the fight. Too often we want God to just fix everything but that only spoils us and does nothing to build spiritual character and that type of character was what I lacked most in my life. The same is true with parents and children when we find ourselves serving in the role of "fixer" instead of being a teacher and an example for them to follow. We need to teach our children to take part in the fight for the things they want and need but I was always guilty of fighting in their place.

I will argue till my last breath that God has a sense of humor! Right in the midst of what appeared to be a marriage dissolving, God does nothing in helping me fight the lies and accusations; He simply tells me I need to work on my spiritual character. People had told me since I was saved at seventeen years old that I was supposed to be a Pastor. I not only told them they were wrong but I often questioned their sanity in saying such a thing! I always wanted to preach and I tell people it took me six years to talk God into letting me get behind a pulpit and once He agreed, I was willing to go anywhere to declare the gospel. The only problem was the phone wasn't ringing and so, that's one reason we started the music ministry with Millie's family. When that ended, we committed to the New Vision Church and I was able to speak there from time to time. But now, while praying for God to save my marriage, He tells me it's time for me to move into a more active ministry role as, you guessed it, a Pastor! My heart melted when in a micro-second the rejection of such a thought left me and all at once my greatest desire was to lead a portion of God's flock. I was forty years old, unsure as to how this attack on our marriage would end and yet God is speaking of the future. I got on board with His idea, He moved the mountains and let light and truth be revealed and the next thing you know, Millie and I are discussing moving into a new level in ministry. It's funny now, but God wasn't worried at all! Imagine that!

By now it is the winter of 1999 and we decided the first step I should take is to begin the process of obtaining a minister's license. Our church was part of the International Pentecostal Holiness Church, IPHC; and so it was the logical next move to contact them about the necessities of obtaining a license. I won't bore you with the logistics of the process but there were three levels of ministry awarded to eligible candidates; a local ministry license where a candidate served under an established Pastor, a level of ministry license which allowed a candidate to Pastor a church which led to the third level of licensing identified as ordination. All three levels required classes be taken and tests given with license's being awarded once a year in June. I only had time that year to obtain the local ministry license but I immediately continued on to receive a regular minister's license which was awarded to me in June of 2000. Eager as a beaver, I also immediately began my ordination process which would take a minimum of two years and so I became a licensed and ordained minister of the IPHC in June of 2002. Thank you Jesus!

Matt had graduated high school in June of 2000 and was preparing to enter a local college on an academic scholarship he had earned with his ACT score. Millie had changed jobs and was working as a secretary in the county school system and I was the director of a local Consumer Credit Counseling office. Josh and Melissa were progressing well in North Dakota and Josh's intelligence and creativity was being noticed by his supervisors and he was receiving commendations for his efforts. Melissa had taken over management of a small motel just outside of Grand Forks and they had relocated and were staying in the living quarters of the motel.

It was a hot day in July, 2000 when the phone rang and the secretary from the Appalachian Conference of the IPHC called and told me the Conference Superintendent suggested I submit my resume' to a church in Wythe County, Virginia for consideration as their next Pastor. I told Millie about it and we decided it would at least be an opportunity to find out how the process works and the information we gained from the experience would help us when the time came for us to actually make such a move.

Remember the God, sense of humor comment? Before I knew it we were leaving our jobs and moving into a parsonage in Austinville, Virginia! It happened so fast I didn't have time to talk God out of it and so I was in my first pulpit. God help me! God help them!

I have heard soldiers talk about getting killed in Vietnam and they didn't even know it. Of course they were referring to being poisoned by chemical warfare which took years to manifest itself in various types of cancer. Millions were walking around with a death sentence already on countdown and wasn't even aware they were sick. So sad the number of soldiers who sank into depression and couldn't handle what they had seen and been a part of in that war who eventually took their own lives to end the suffering. Thank you Lord for grace that is greater than all our sin!

Josh was killed in North Dakota and didn't even know it. No, there wasn't an invasion from Canada where chemical weapons were used but his poison proved just as deadly as you will see as this story unfolds. It wasn't agent orange; it was asbestos. Life is sometimes filled with irony and it often makes things more difficult to understand. The base clinic Josh worked in was being renovated and the military employees who served there decided to get involved in an effort to hold costs down. They performed some of the demolition and the local newspaper ran a story on the project to boost public relations for the base. They printed a picture of an Airman up on a step ladder with his head and hands in the ceiling removing the old tiles. The Airman of course was Josh and unknown at the time, the ceiling tiles contained asbestos. It wasn't enough to kill someone quickly mind you, but it was enough to inflame the sinuses of someone who already suffered from sinus difficulty. You guessed it, Josh developed a bad sinus condition afterwards and the funny thing is that very picture was available as evidence when Josh was awarded partial veteran's disability and we actually still have it.

It was one of those things that just happened and nobody was really at fault, especially the volunteer demolition crew. We all have experienced such defining moments in our lives where our future was altered and perhaps we didn't even notice it. Maybe it was a decision to take a different college class which ultimately led us to an unexpected career choice. Perhaps we simply zigged instead of zagging and here we are. However, when a defining moment in your life affects your health in a negative way, you are robbed of a better and brighter future which may have been your destiny. We never know how things might have ended up without such a defining moment of change, but we can't help but wonder what could have been if Josh hadn't been exposed to the asbestos.

CHAPTER 8

Coming Home

It was now late in the year 2000, Y2K had been a dud and we were ministering in our new church while preparing to relocate to the community and live in the church parsonage. The church was only about seventy five minutes from our home in WV but it seemed like we were moving across country. We were nervous and excited at the same time but we kept our eyes on the prize. Matt was in his first semester of college but chose to relocate with us rather than stay in school and live with grandparents. We were glad to have him but his decision led him to some personal struggles but he was able to overcome them and became fairly active with us in the church. Josh and Melissa had entered their fourth year of the Air Force and what to do next was weighing heavily on their minds.

The year 2000 also brought with it some exciting times for them as Josh was awarded Airman of the Quarter for the first three months of the year. It was a great honor that also included commendations and even a few prizes. As I said before, Josh was very intelligent and had a strong work ethic and it was evident in what he accomplished while in the military. At the end of the year, the Airmen who won the award for each of the four quarters was eligible to become Airman of the Year for Grand Forks Air Force Base and Josh received that prestigious honor as well. There was talk that he now would be eligible for consideration as a Pentagon internship if interested, which would last for one year.

To be considered, Josh would have to re-enlist since his four years would be up in June of 2001 and he most likely wouldn't find out if he was chosen until after his re-enlistment was effective. They both were homesick and wanted to move back home so together, they made the choice to leave the Air Force and return to Southern West Virginia to find work and settle down. I have no idea how many times he said leaving the Air Force was the greatest mistake of his life but we have no way of knowing if that was correct. In light of how things turned out, it seems like it would have been the best decision to re-enlist but hindsight is always twenty-twenty.

We had been unable to sell our home since moving into the parsonage, so when Josh and Melissa offered to buy it, we gave it much consideration. We agreed that they would rent for one year and if they still wanted it, we would reduce the price by the rent they had paid and that is exactly what happened. Josh had placed a job application with the veteran's hospital in Beckley, West Virginia, and was granted an interview. However, they told him the waiting list for employment was long and sometimes applicants would wait for a year until a position opened. Josh was undoubtedly discouraged but the discouragement didn't last long for when they reviewed his application and resume', they called the next day and offered him a position. The administration had high hopes for him and he met and exceeded their expectations in job performance and seemed to be on a fast track for promotions.

Melissa had found work as well and the pieces of their new lives were coming together. They started back attending the church they were married in and even worked with the youth for a while. Sometimes they were able to visit us in Austinville and attend services there. Josh would play drums and Melissa would help Millie lead singing. I played the piano and Matt was learning the bass guitar so it was a family affair and we loved it! Things were going well for all of us and did so for quite a while. We had bumps in the road and challenges to face but all in all, it was a good season for all of us and one we are grateful to God for it because when it changed, it really changed.

The last twelve or so years and are much like a blur with events and situations all running together and that is why I cannot remember the exact day Josh died. I won't try to assign times and dates to the rest of my story until the end because to me, it seems like one long, long, long day. I guess I better explain what I meant when I said I can't remember the day when Josh died. I am referring to the Josh we all knew and loved up to that point; the smart, occasionally depressed, wise decision making, artistic and hard working Josh who was respected, loved and admired by many.

I was there that day, it was just me and him because everyone else had to work and I had the flexibility as Pastor to take him to the hospital. It was supposed to be a routine sinus surgery to open up his passages which had been inflamed by the asbestos. He struggled to get a deep breath and lived on nasal spray medication and the battle to get good oxygen often resulted in migraine headaches which left him incapacitated for hours. This surgery was supposed to fix all those issues and help him to breathe normally and even though he was a smoker, it was the inflamed sinus passages which gave him the most difficulty breathing.

We were at the veteran's hospital where he was an employee so he was getting the red carpet treatment. Everyone was so nice and friendly and checked on him regularly throughout the day and we felt we had no need to have any concerns. It was a minor surgery and the doctor had performed it many times with just as many successes. But this time the result was different because they couldn't open up the sinuses as they had hoped and the procedure had left Josh in unbelievable pain and of course, a migraine. Instead of going home that afternoon he was admitted to the hospital for overnight observation and given medication for the pain.

If I had been listening closely, I may have heard taps being played in the background and I had no idea that he was experiencing a second, life altering, defining moment in his life. I remember very clearly the tears I shed and the prayers I prayed while standing over him that day. If I could have taken his place I would have, and it was so difficult to watch him lay there in that bed and suffer such pain. The pain medication, taken by millions every day with no bad side effects, awakened an addiction in our son that neither he, us, or anyone else on this earth knew was in there. The Josh I took to the hospital died and a new Josh was born; we just didn't know it yet and we had no idea what awaited him and the rest of us as this evil addiction usurped authority in his life. Josh once shared with me that as he took the pain medication in the days following the surgery, he realized the more often he took them, the less pain he had and the better he felt. I guess in many ways that could be the opening sentence in the testimony of any addict.

The Bible says the serpent approached Eve in the Garden of Eden in a subtle manner. In other words, his intentions weren't realized until after the forbidden fruit was eaten. In much the same way, Josh knew a change had occurred in him but it was a subtle one and he didn't realize it until it had a strong hold on him. Now please understand, I am not making excuses for the poor decisions he made in the months and years following his surgery, I am only saying that this issue, which may never be a problem for you and your family, is a real disease with devastating consequences. I have taken pain medication with no problem, Millie has done the same but there was something in Josh's anatomy that grabbed it, liked it, and wanted more of it. I don't understand it all but watching my son fight for his life for so many years has convinced me it is real and I will not deny it or remain silent about it.

Josh's experience has proven to me that mental illness, addiction and clinical depression are all diseases just like cancer or any other destructive illness. That being said, I know these diseases can be healed by the hand of a Sovereign God and I have heard the testimonies from individuals who have experienced such divine interventions in their lives. But, I also know that many haven't been healed and I am not bold enough to point the finger at them and tell them they are the reason their healing didn't come. Maybe you are, but not me. Gradually, Josh became deeply depressed from the lack of understanding why he wasn't healed. There were times when groups of young people from successful rehabilitation facilities would share their testimonies in church of how God had delivered them, but eventually, Josh wouldn't go to hear them because it never happened for him and their stories actually discouraged him. It saddens me to know there are so many others out there who feel there is no hope for them just like Josh felt.

People mean well, I know they do, but have you ever noticed that the one person who tells you to trust God when you need a job is the same person that has a good job already? Everybody seems to have an answer for every problem as long as they are someone else's problems but it is a different story when the problem sets up occupancy in your home. We had been told we needed more faith but I don't think that was the problem. Some have said you haven't prayed enough or you haven't given the problem to God yet. Sounds good but I don't think so. Some even said Josh lacked faith and it makes me wonder if there is some kind of faith gauge we haven't discovered? We had faith, we prayed, we gave the problem to God, heck, we even gave Josh to God but for whatever reason we couldn't find the path to victory in Josh's addiction problem. I can hear the grumblings already in the hearts of those who disagree but that's okay, I know what we did, how we prayed and trusted but I also am living the rest of the story as well.

When Josh couldn't sleep at night he often watched late night televangelism and believed for a season what he heard concerning certain teaching on giving and receiving. Now we all know how generous God is and how He delights in giving to His children, but I didn't believe then, and neither do I now, that God's miracles are for sale. There, I said it and lightning didn't strike me. If miracles were for sale Josh surely would have bought one because he would literally give the shirt off his back. He had done it before and I have seen him do it. He was the guy who would have a twenty dollar restaurant bill and because the waitress was a young single mom, would leave a fifty dollar tip. There was one time a waitress actually chased him outside thinking he made a mistake and he told her what she found on the table was hers.

Now he also had the tendency to sometimes tell us what he did but still, he was the most generous person I have ever met and even today, we are still blessing others with the few things he left behind. My point is this, Josh prayed, he sought wisdom and help from others he determined qualified to provide it, he did what we all have done. Let's be honest, there have been times we have thought that if we do enough God things, then God will do things for us. Of course, actions like that eliminate grace which is given to all apart from works but still, we all are guilty of trying to help God help us.

CHAPTER 9

The Downward Spiral

I have a riddle for you; "What do you get when you cross an over-achieving perfectionist with a guilt ridden soul addicted to prescription pain pills?" Give up? You get a self-destructive person living with a deep secret that causes them to helplessly spiral downward into deep depression. Josh was his own worst enemy insomuch as he knew what he was doing was wrong and the guilt he felt, not just from the addiction but also the lies necessary to hide it, destroyed his self confidence and his self esteem. Consequently, a new Josh emerged and it took most of us quite a while to recognize it. As I said before, I will not provide times and dates for all the battles we all went through after that surgery, but I will just try to let my heart speak to the things that stand out to me. I hope, and I deeply pray that as I reveal the inward parts of this journey, that there are some folks out there who can identify with what I say and seek for help and guidance in how to navigate through their own journey.

When the depression deepened, really became noticeable and started manifesting in emotional problems, we would go to meet with the counselors the Veteran's Administration had assigned to Josh. They were helpful to us and showed general concern for Josh at first, but he ended up on large amounts of various medications as they attempted to cure him chemically. At one point, between his primary care physician and his psychiatrist, Josh was on twenty six different medications but it only made matters worse and we noticed right away that he had developed the ability to tell professionals exactly what they wanted to hear in order to get what he wanted. That cute behavior he used to demonstrate as a child to get himself out of trouble had now become his primary weapon in justifying his issues.

As his dad, the family looked to me for leadership and guidance as to how to handle each event and being the passive, enabler that I am, I came up short. I should have jumped up on the table and screamed "no more!" Not just to the counselors and physicians, but particularly to Josh because his words would manipulate me and cause me to believe it would be different next time. But, it was always the same and he would continually work things around for his benefit. No matter how many times he was on suicide watch in some emergency department or just saying he and everyone else would be better off if he was dead, I would search for one hopeful thought to hang onto so I could ignore the impending disaster. Looking back now, I think we all recognized what he was doing but were afraid to admit it to others and to ourselves. I am reminded of how someone once defined insanity as doing the same things over and over but expecting a different result. That is the mindset of an enabler in a nutshell.

Sadly, Josh wasn't our family's first experience with the lies and addiction. Millie's youngest brother Steve, fought drug addiction and told his share of lies as he lost everything as a result of his lifestyle. His decision to end his own life at age twenty eight still breaks the hearts of family members and robbed his mother of her smile up until her own death. He served as an example to the other children in the family and Josh often said he didn't want to follow the same path as uncle Steve, yet he found himself in the exact same self destructing journey.

If you have a loved one who is doing the same thing, please take my advice and be pro-active and not passive in your actions toward them. Trust me, it will not get better on its own and the losers in the end will be everyone in your family. Addiction produces a competent liar and believe me, they become very good at it. I think it may be one of the first, if not the very first sign you will see when addiction of any kind has bitten someone you love. Eventually the lies will tell on them as they can't remember what they have said or promised, but by then a great deal of damage may have been done. I saw so many things in Josh that I will finish my life in regret because I was passive and failed to confront him on his lies and his addiction. I would treasure the peace and joy of having him safely in front

43

of me for a few moments and temporarily forget the lies and manipulation. No one wins if truth does not prevail.

With that said, every time Josh would try to abandon the pills, his life would sink into deep depression which began to leave him suicidal. He was either flying high on the pills or living low in the depression. The doctors began treating him more aggressively for the depression and it helped when he would stay on the medications but Josh had this belief that taking medication was wrong, with no exceptions. His soon to be diagnosed bi-polar disorder explained why he felt this way but at this time he was basing it on what he was hearing on late night television. He operated from one extreme to the other and nothing any of us could say or do made any difference whatsoever. I have searched my life to see if I could have contributed to his warped belief system but I can't find a time where he could have concluded those thoughts from what I said or did. Nonetheless, the beliefs were real to him and just as soon as the meds brought him to a place of stability, he would begin contemplating what a failure he was for taking them and unjustified guilt would overtake him. He would stop cold turkey and the downward spiral started all over again. This happened again and again with different medications which were prescribed to help him gain stability. Stability brought guilt, guilt brought ill advised decisions to drop medications, bad decisions brought deep depression, and the depression brought suicidal tendencies which once again brought medications to bring him stability. I think you understand what I am saying.

Let me add this on Josh's behalf. There were times over the last twelve or so years that Josh functioned and lived a healthy, sober life and was blessed to enjoy many wonderful things. Although, he eventually left his job at the veteran's hospital, he was blessed to go back to college where he was able to take an art class and expand his God-given talent of drawing. He had received a partial veteran's disability award and so the college was paid for and he also received a monthly disability check. He was blessed to take vacations and develop skills and talents that otherwise would have been unrealized. His love of music led him to learn how to play and record multiple instruments and he even made a tape of songs in which he was the only musician! He played drums in church and even publically with secular groups from time to time. He was a different person when holding drum sticks and bringing the beat of the music to listening ears gave him a great sense of accomplishment.

We took trips together, laughed together and had as much enjoyment as most other families, so the entire time was not without meaning and purpose. Even though they never had children, Josh and Melissa had many pets from time to time which he loved and cared for just like you would a child. They brought many hours of joy and satisfaction to him and they would always have what he thought they needed whether he had what he needed or not. He actually closed in the front porch of their home and put in an air conditioner and heater for the cats so they could enjoy all the comforts he and Melissa did. However, the greatest joy of Josh's life was born just a few years ago to Melissa's sister Angie and her husband Jamie. Little Riley Baldwin had Josh's heart from day one and he loved her like she was his own. After he had been one hundred percent disabled by the Veteran's Administration, Josh often said that maybe God had blessed him with such a good income to always make sure Riley would have what she needed and had he lived, he would have done just that. Of course her mom, dad, Grandma Cathy and Aunt Melissa will do that anyway but Josh had sure volunteered for the job.

Josh had an uncanny sense of humor which would manifest itself at the most unusual times. When he said something funny, it really was funny and he could make you laugh until your sides hurt. He loved deep, philosophical discussions and could presents sides of issues most would never consider. He cared deeply for people but found it difficult to be around suffering and hurting people unless he could do something to help them. He possessed many compassionate characteristics and they defined who he really was.

I felt it necessary to insert above comments for two reasons; one, so you will know that Josh did have seasons of success and happiness in his struggle and two, so you will not have false hope if your loved one does the same. Remember, addiction is a killer disease and just doesn't go away on its own. It must be defeated or it will manifest again and again with each time more costly than before. So many times our hopes for him were crushed as a season of good times would abruptly end with the addiction and depression emerging more determined than ever to destroy him.

I was serving Holy Communion at church one Sunday morning when

I noticed someone come to the front to get Millie to answer a phone call to the church. It was Melissa telling us Josh had tried to commit suicide and was in the hospital emergency room. We left the church and headed to the hospital and I don't think Millie, Matt or myself even said a word to each other the entire hour required for the trip. We did not know what we would find when we arrived and we had tried to prepare ourselves but it was like a bad dream. We had heard the threats before and been with him in isolation in the emergency department but now he had actually tried it. He had arrived at the hospital in time with no serious damage to his body but the rest of us lost years from our lives; or at least it seemed like it.

That was the first time I realized how helpless I was to beat this problem for him. Many years ago I was given a "dads prayer coin" by our Men's Ministries group and I faithfully carried it with me everywhere I went and I still do. Stepping away from the emergency department for a moment I took my car keys from my pocket and that prayer coin came out with them and landed on the ground. I bent down to pick it up when I noticed four words in bold print looking back up in me. Just like any other coin in my pocket, the prayer coin also said these words; "IN GOD WE TRUST." I found great comfort from those words and held to them from that point on. Of course, I was like most parents, I claimed to trust God as long as I could help Him along!

I don't know how many trips we made to the veteran's hospital, clinics and rehab facilities for counseling sessions or to meet with one of his doctors, but they were more than a few and always ended the same with Josh promising better behavior and us believing him. No matter the problem, one call and dad came running; not with solutions which I was incapable of having, but just to be someone to fix what Josh wanted. Whatever the need, dad could fix it. I couldn't take his addiction away but I sure became proficient in keeping it going. I just didn't know that was what I was doing. I bet there are many others who are doing the same thing while all along think they are helping. A simple truth seemed to escape me; fueling a fire only makes it burn hotter.

CHAPTER 10

Will Things Ever be Better?

When our kids learned to drive I spent a lot of time holding my breath when the phone rang. Those were the days before cell phones and caller ID so when either son was out in a car and I answered an unexpected call, I did so with great dread as to who the voice would be at the other end of the line. I always said that the only thing worse than receiving a wrong number phone call at four a.m., is receiving a right number phone call at that time. I loved Josh with all my heart and still do, but as I said before, driving a car was not his greatest talent. Once when he was a teenager I was called to an accident site to witness rescue workers using the "jaws of life" emergency equipment to remove him from our car. He wasn't seriously injured but it was enough to make my heart stop for a moment. He was constantly backing into this and bumping into that with whatever he was driving and of course, there was always a reason he would offer. We would just accredit it to the fact he was never going to be a great driver and hopefully, he wouldn't be seriously injured or be the cause of someone else's serious injury. As I sit here and look back over the years I can only be grateful to God that none of his accidents resulted in physical harm to anyone other than himself.

I am neither qualified nor capable of passing judgment on the causes of some of his automobile accidents but I will admit that I do wonder how many of the minor ones may have been intentional in order to get pain medications. We had no books on the behaviors of addicts which we could refer to and at that time, we still thought the entire struggle in his life was spiritual and would never consider such a thought of him having a disease.

If you ask me though, I don't think it much matters. I mean if someone has a problem, be it spiritual or physical, it is all the result of the fall of man in the Garden of Eden which brought the consequences of original sin into this world. I don't think the person with the problem cares as much about the cause as they do the cure. That may not be a very spiritual attitude to take but I am reminded of something Josh once said to me in one of his good periods. We were talking about the Bible and he said; "It is hard to make people care about a hell in the afterlife when they are already living in one now." Is it possible that we as the Church of the Risen Savior have become so disconnected from the world in which we are called to minister, that we fail to see the pain and suffering so many around us endure each day? Are we so consumed with attending church that we forget to be the church? Have we forgotten that we are "His Body" and we must interact with those who need Him? God help us all!

It was around five p.m. one afternoon and we had made the trip back home from Austinville to visit with parents and Millie and I were at my mom and dad's house when the phone rang. Josh was on the other end trying to find us. Apparently, someone had been traveling north in the southbound lanes of I-77 as Josh was coming home from work and caused to him to veer into the rear of a tractor-trailer truck and wreck his vehicle. We made the trip to the veteran's hospital where he worked because the ambulance had taken him there. Thankfully, he was okay except the doctor said he had a small fracture in his pelvic bone which would heal with time. He was to take it easy for a few days and take the prescribed pain medication as needed. No problem, right?

Later on, Josh was diagnosed with a mild case of Crohn's disease of which the treatment mainly involved some type of steroid medication. Little did we know at the time, but the steroids weakened the fracture in his pelvic bone and led to hip replacement at age thirty five. This crushed his self esteem because it led to total disability after already causing him to lose his job at the Social Security Administration which he obtained after leaving the veteran's hospital. Together, we had all concluded it may be best for him to change occupational environments and get a new start away from his current environment.

It wasn't just the addiction and depression that concerned us, Josh felt like he had to save everyone who came in with a problem and when he couldn't, it really took a toll on him. God had graciously opened a door for him at the SSA but a flare up of the Crohn's caused him to unexpectedly miss work during his training period. After returning to work, they started his training over but again, the Crohn's flared up again and he missed more work. They suggested that due to all his health issues, he should apply for disability through Civil Service which he was awarded almost immediately and the hip surgery came soon after. He was a talented and skilled, thirty five year old man who would most likely never be able to work publicly again. The depression deepened and the addiction grew worse and as the addiction grew worse, the depression deepened. I think you get the picture. We had begun to wonder if things would ever be better.

One of Josh's accidents involved flipping a new Ford Ranger he had bought while working at the veteran's hospital. Miraculously, he suffered only minor injuries but the truck wasn't so lucky; it was a total loss. He and Melissa had good credit and good income so replacing a vehicle was never a difficult task and sometimes he would make an emotional decision such as the time he bought a Ford Mustang. He always wanted one but it was more than he could afford so he eventually lost it.

Josh was once a great steward of their finances but as he battled the depression and addiction he often made poor decisions which left their finances in a mess. Together, their combined incomes were actually greater than Millie's and mine were but there were multiple times he would call for a small loan or some other type of financial help. If we had it, I gave it to him. If we didn't, I often borrowed it myself and let him make the payments. What I didn't know, or even want to consider was the fact he was using his income to support his habit and that was leaving them short each month for bills and living expenses. This wasn't an every month experience because as I said before, Josh had many good seasons of healthy, happy living but the darkness of depression and addiction was always waiting for him to return, and sadly, he always did.

I don't know how many times and how many facilities Josh went for help with his problems. There were multiple hospitals he was admitted to for treatment for his mental illness and depression. Several trips to rehab facilities to try to break free from his addiction, some of which our families didn't know about and most of which our friends and church families never knew about. Pastoral counseling, clinical counseling, prayer, you name it, we did it all in an effort to see our beloved Josh break free from this stronghold on his life. We shed tears, tried to make deals with God and would have mortgaged ourselves to the max if we could have found a place to get him help. There was a season in which Millie and I called every night before bedtime to pray with him to have the strength to get through the next day. It was heart-wrenching to watch someone you love suffer as he did and not be able to get them the help needed to set them free. As long as someone wants help, you can at least move forward in searching but when they give up it becomes a different story. We just kept hoping he wouldn't give up because we knew with his personality, it wouldn't end well.

Giving up would certainly be a major problem but it seemed the greatest problem was Josh's tendency to give in. He not only gave in to the cravings of the addiction and the darkness of the depression, he would also give in to untested and unproven solutions. I guess the worst decision he ever made in his entire struggle was to try methadone to get off the drugs he was taking. I didn't know anything about methadone but he sounded like a brochure when he told me how it would help him recover and so I thought it was a good idea. Wrong! Come to find out, he was abandoning an illegal drug habit only to start a legal one. The methadone was expensive and not covered by insurance plus he had to drive almost one hour every day just to get to the closest clinic. Many of the unfortunate events in his life I have discussed happened while he was a patient at the methadone clinic. If you know someone who is trapped in the methadone lie, please do all you can to change the path of their recovery effort. methadone clinics are often places where addicts come in contact with resources for other illicit drug use and can be a source of friendships which only add to the problems. Such was the case with Josh.

There were other attempts to take his life but some were mostly talk and we sort of became numb to it. People told us that the person who always talks about suicide is the one least likely to try it. In some twisted way, it was actually comforting to think like that. One time he took some pills and then called 911 himself. I think he was reaching out for help in some way but I can't be sure. He lived with such guilt over his life choices and nothing you could ever say would give him any sense of self worth. The doctors would have him on certain medicines that shouldn't be stopped abruptly, but that's exactly what he would do. It wreaked havoc on his body and would mentally make him an entirely different person. He would spend days and hours alone and we constantly encouraged him to get out of the house and be a volunteer at something which would give him social contacts. He knew it was a good idea but always found a reason to not do it which left us frustrated and often angry at him. So much of his complaints could have been corrected if he had just allowed someone else's advice to influence him, but once he set his mind a certain way, there was no changing it.

I guess only Melissa and God know for sure how many incidents, how many critical moments and how many victories and defeats Josh actually experienced. I know she shared most but I also know she kept some to herself as she learned to live with a bi-polar addict who suffered from depression. We felt the need to be closer to home not only for Josh, but we still had all four of our parents with us and we needed to be more involved in their personal care and well being as each of them were aging. So, I resigned from the church in Austinville, Virginia and took a church in Narrows, Virginia which was about forty five minutes closer to home. We could now check on Josh and our families more often and were actually close enough to have more family interaction. The church was called Cornerstone Church and the people were a loving group and I feel like we immediately developed lasting relationships with them. Time has proven that to be true and we stayed there for eight and one half years as Pastor.

Millie and I were on our way to the mall in Christiansburg, Virginia one Saturday morning when Melissa called to tell us Josh was unresponsive on the couch and she had called 911. He had slept on the couch the night before and she thought he was just sleeping when she tried to awaken him just before noon. We immediately turned around and headed to Princeton, West Virginia to the hospital emergency department. God is amazing to say the least! The little area we had moved from which Josh and Melissa had moved to after leaving the Air Force, had developed some drug abuse issues and that's all I will say about it. It was definitely not an ideal place for Josh to be and he had become swallowed up by it to say the least.

One evening Millie went to our church for some private prayer time and her focus was on God selling their house for them so they could move. The next morning, a neighbor offered Josh the amount he and Melissa wanted for the house and could pay it in cash! I will not speculate how someone had that much cash in a brown paper bag but we were celebrating the fact they could move away. Now it was Saturday and Josh had tried to take his life again but this time, it looked like he might have succeeded. We arrived to find him unconscious and the emergency staff had started treatments to counteract the drugs he had taken. The doctor said he was going to induce a medical coma and put Josh on a ventilator to allow his body to recover.

He was in the intensive care unit for several days before being awakened and taken off the ventilator and thank God, he had no consequences from the overdose and went straight to a mental help facility to continue his recovery. Josh had beaten the methadone treatment once and came completely off of it. However, he eventually slipped backward and entered methadone treatment a second time and it eventually controlled everything he did because it required attention every day. He hated the fact that he could never have a normal day because it always started with a trip to be "dosed" as he called it. Sadly, he never made it off the treatment a second time.

After this ordeal, Josh had a good year or more of healthy living and during that time he engaged himself in more things outside of the home which made us all very happy. He and Melissa eventually started going to a church in their community and he ended up playing the drums for them. Josh always had a strong faith and even in his darkest periods of failure, he would acknowledge the power and grace of God. There are people today who have an active relationship with Jesus Christ because Josh took the time to tell them about the love God has for them. It is ironic that someone who couldn't find peace pointed others to the Cross of Calvary where they could find peace.

We had many deep discussions on topics from the Bible and I must admit there were times he made me think and search the scriptures. There was no denying the Presence of God in his life even though his journey was not the one Christ chose for him. Thank you Lord for Your Amazing Grace! Also, after this attempt at suicide, I made the decision to provide full disclosure concerning what we as a family were going through. When I requested prayer at church the morning following the suicide attempt, I told them exactly what was wrong and what had happened. Trying to hide such things may reduce some measure of embarrassment but revealing them provides a freedom that only personal experience can explain.

We have found that there will always be some people who cast judgment on everything and everybody. When you have a family member who is an addict and has attempted suicide, such people come out of the woodwork to gossip their opinions and accusations. Even as our son lay in his coffin on the night of his funeral there were some who spread false stories about what had happened even though we were totally open and honest about it. But, for the most part, people, especially God's people, are kind and compassionate and non-judgmental and really go out of their way to support and love others who are going through what we did. That is what we experienced; the immeasurable love of God demonstrated through the actions of so many who reached out to us in our darkest hour. Glory to His Name!

CHAPTER 11

The Prodigal Returns

I could fill page after page if I tried to include every up and down moment of the last twelve plus years, but hopefully I have shared enough so far to impress upon you the urgency of how any ordinary son or daughter can face what Josh faced. The remainder of this book will share the story of the final chapter of our son's life. In 2014, Millie had expressed her wishes that we have a family vacation in the summer of 2015. We were going to provide everything for Josh, Melissa, Matt and ourselves to spend a week at the beach. The reservations were made and paid for and all we needed was for summer to arrive. Just prior to the scheduled vacation, Josh tested positive for some type of unaccepted drug during a random test at the methadone clinic so he was unable to get the "take home doses" he had earned for the trip. He tried to arrange treatment from a clinic near the beach but they wouldn't accept him because of the failed drug test. Nothing could be done so he and Melissa were unable to take the vacation trip with us.

After we returned from the beach, his probationary period had ended so we gave them spending money for them to take a little trip by themselves. By then, he was able to receive treatment from a clinic near their vacation destination, and they were able to get away for a few days. I don't know what happened, where it happened or how it happened, but soon afterwards a change was evident in Josh. I can't explain it but he just wasn't the same. We had become accustomed to his mood swings caused by the depression and addiction, but this was different and we couldn't explain it. It was as if some part of his mind had shut down and his actions became increasingly irrational.

I had been feeling disconnected in my spirit from Cornerstone Church and I still don't have a good explanation as to why. The church was doing okay and we had been able to bring a lot of improvements and updates to the facility. God had blessed us to get out of debt and the church was operating in the black with a strong support of missions around the world and locally. I guess I just felt like my purpose there had ended. No one agreed with the decision and I think the church was generally disappointed, but I felt it in my spirit so I announced my resignation to be effective the first Sunday in October, 2015. Now, nearly a year later, I still can't find a viewpoint where my decisions make sense to me and perhaps the unsettledness I felt was for what was coming. All I know is I have been unable to make even the simplest of decisions over the last several months without being filled with doubt and even fear and I find myself mostly feeling lost and alone. It could just be this gaping hole in my heart I have since we lost our son.

Just a couple of weeks before my final Sunday at the church, something had snapped with Josh and he went off the deep end to say the least. He unexpectedly left Melissa, emptied their bank account and maxed out their credit cards for a few days of excessive partying. It was like the prodigal son in the Bible who wasted all he had on "riotous living." Out of respect for Melissa and Millie I won't go into details but Josh made a lot of bad decisions in just a very short time. We knew their marriage wasn't perfect, but whose is? However, Melissa was always the strong end of the bungee cord which Josh was attached too and she always was there to snap him back to reality. Now that he had severed that cord, he had cut off the most stable factor he had in his life. His money spent, accountability severed, and used up by so-called friends he literally had nothing left and nowhere to go.

We went for several days not knowing where he was, who he was with and what he was doing; we only knew he was leaving a trail of poor judgment in his wake. Millie and I were sitting in our living room one afternoon when I told her there was no way this could end well. Matt knew we were worried and upset so he went to look for him. He found him at one of Josh's friend's house and begged him to come home with him. Josh was in bad shape and said some very ugly things about Matt and us and so Matt came home a bit upset. When the dust settled, Josh rented a mobile home and asked me to help him move the few things he wanted from his eighteen year marriage into his new place. Now understand this, Melissa would have given him anything he asked for but he was insistent she keep all the major items so she could have what she needed. He only lived in the mobile home for a short time when his new friends robbed him and took what valuables he had left plus his cash. I hope that is what happened even though I realize some or all of it could just be a fabrication.

Punkin came into our lives the second or third year we were at Austinville. She was an abandoned kitten who showed up half starved at our back door where Matt found her. To make a long story short, she soon ended up with the run of our home and I will admit, I loved her dearly. She moved with us from Austinville, with a brief stop in Dublin, Virginia and then to Narrows where by now, she was Queen Punkin. What does a silly cat have to do with my story? Well, my last day at Cornerstone Church was Sunday, October 4, and Punkin died on Tuesday, October 6 from complications of anesthesia while getting some teeth pulled. We had already endured enough sadness in the eight and one half years we were at Cornerstone. Of course it had nothing to do with the church but we had lost Millie's dad in 2009, her mom in 2011, my dad in 2014 and now Punkin. I wept uncontrollably and I am not embarrassed to admit it. She was my therapy for all those years and I was going to miss her terribly. Earlier that morning Matt went to check on Josh and found him in a bad way. Concerned he might harm himself, Matt had loaded everything he had into the truck Josh had just bought and paid a fortune for, and was bringing him to our home where he would at least be safe, fed and warm.

Of course, the truck had been wrecked and it was scheduled for repairs in Christiansburg and his insurance planned to provide him a rental car. He was still a patient at the methadone clinic near Beckley, West Virginia so every morning he would drive the seventy five minutes up there and the same seventy five minutes back to our home in Narrows. He was broke and Millie and I had to cover the cost of the methadone and the trips up there and back, but we did so by giving him the money he needed on a daily basis and not all at once. At least he was able to show some responsibility and was held accountable, so, as long as he came back home each day, he had the opportunity to have a stable environment.

It was nearly impossible to get any real information from him as to why he had abandoned his eighteen year marriage and fell into such a trap of bad decision making. He had his reasons and of course, some made sense and some didn't. I can't explain it and I certainly won't try to defend his behavior. Every time we tried to have a conversation with him about what was going on, he would get angry, storm out of the room and threaten to leave. He did share with us that the night before he left from the home he and Melissa shared as husband and wife, he sat on the couch with a pistol in his mouth, tears streaming from his eyes while trying to find the courage to pull the trigger. He said he knew he was a disappointment to everyone and felt things would be better if he was out of the picture. We tried to assure him that was certainly not the case but he wouldn't listen.

With no family ties in the Narrows, Virginia area, we decided to put our home up for sale and move to the next county where Millie was employed as a sixth grade Language Arts teacher. I was employed by the Giles County School system as a bus driver and planned to travel back each day so I could keep my job. We listed our home with a realtor one Thursday and the lady who eventually bought it looked at it the next Thursday. She made an offer we accepted so now, just two weeks from my last Sunday at the church, we had to make plans to move. There was a methadone clinic within fifteen minutes of the home we found to rent so it made perfect sense that upon moving, we would all have a chance to start over. We started packing and after moving a few items in advance we planned the big move for the Saturday after Thanksgiving which would be November 30. The deal on our home was scheduled to close on the following Tuesday so everything seemed to be God's perfect timing. Josh had expressed excitement for the fresh start and we were all looking forward to getting settled in the new place. We even sat around and talked about how he would be in a new town and no one would know his history so maybe he could get his troubles straightened out.

Saturday morning arrived and I had rented the largest U-haul truck I could get and family, plus folks from Cornerstone showed up to help us load and move. Josh had left early for the clinic but had not returned when expected. By now his truck had been repaired but he had taken Matt's car and left the truck for us to use for the move. It was about noon when my cell phone rang and the caller ID showed the call coming from Josh's cell phone. I answered the phone but did not recognize the voice on the other end, however, the caller proceeded to tell me who he was and that Josh was with him. It seemed that Josh didn't want to relocate after all and was choosing to remain with his friend who lived near the methadone clinic in West Virginia. Of course his friend was also receiving treatments but he assured us Josh would be okay with him and would be staying with him and his mom in their apartment.

I think if I could have a do-over, I would have demanded Josh get on the phone and that he bring Matt's car home. Maybe then I could have influenced him to go with us but I feared a confrontation and let things go. Besides, we had to move that day and I had no time to waste. I had volunteers on hands with the extra trucks we needed and he was a thirty eight year old man who could make his own decisions so we would make our move without him and hope he would come to his senses and join us. He did not contest Melissa's petition for a divorce and so as I had feared, there was no bungee cord attached that could yank him back into reason. His poor decisions had led him to a whole new place where he would not be safe and I couldn't protect him anymore. He would develop a new social circle filled with people struggling with addiction just as he was and he convinced himself it was his purpose in life to save them. He was determined to contradict the scriptures and prove that the blind could lead the blind and not fall into a ditch but of course, he failed.

Later on Josh said he blamed me because he felt like he was being forced to move and wasn't able to make his own decisions. He was in a position where he needed someone to help him get back on his feet but instead of choosing our help, he thought he could find it from people who were worse off than he was. Naturally, that was impossible and the hole he was in just kept getting deeper and deeper.

CHAPTER 12

Running Out of Time

December came and with it, his monthly disability check. By the fourth day of the month it was gone and he told us someone broke the window out of his truck and robbed him. Later on, his friend said he locked the keys in it and broke the window out to get in. Either way, he was broke, two hours from our home, no food, no gas and apparently nowhere to stay. It seems like the previous mentioned accommodations were no longer available and he was sleeping in his truck. At least that is what he said when he bothered to call us and thankfully, it was an unusually warm December.

We went days at a time without hearing from him and of course we worried and prayed around the clock. Matt and I actually met his friend whom I will leave nameless out of respect for his privacy, and we both thought the guy was legitimate. We later found out otherwise but who knows for sure, most of our information came from Josh and was speculative at best. Josh asked if we could just give him cash for Christmas and we did, so he agreed to spend Christmas Eve with the family even though he slept the whole time. He looked so thin and pale but at least he was with us and everyone was worried and concerned about him.

There was also a young lady Josh became attached to and he felt it was his call in life to redeem her from the darkness of the world she was trapped in. She too, was a patient at the methadone clinic and he quickly became obsessed with her. I will also leave her nameless because it's just not important that I identify anyone when I don't have all the facts. All I know is she had a hold on Josh and he couldn't shake her from his thoughts. He spent all his money on her and her problems and came to me for help when his funds ran out. But, instead of taking care of his business, he spent our money in support of her drug habit as well as his own. Oh yea, did I mention that I have a problem as an enabler? I am embarrassed to mention the actual amount of the several thousand dollars we spent on him and his problems during the last eight months of his life. Finally, he came home in January and he transferred to the methadone clinic near our home and we were encouraged for a short season.

By now he had wrecked his truck again and was in a rental car which he had also wrecked three times. The little Nissan they gave him looked like a bomb went off in it. He had been in multiple accidents in the truck partly because he had broken his glasses and kept rear ending people in addition to keeping all the ice knocked off the guard rails. We had given him money for new glasses but instead, he wasted it on their habits. I took his old glasses and had them repaired so he could at least see where he was going. By then, he had received several traffic violation tickets and for some reason they never took his driver's license away. It had to be obvious he was high because he was always combative when the police pulled him over. I will never be able to figure out why he was allowed to continue driving. With all his accidents over a period of several years no one ever took his license away. Even with all the tickets, he was even allowed to get a Virginia license when he moved here!

Once he moved in with us, things settled down a bit and except for some disagreements in our home, it looked like we were making progress. His unpaid debt had caught up with him and he was unable to keep the truck after it was repaired so he allowed it to be repossessed. Guess who stepped in to save the day? I took him to a dealership which offered a one year lease program regardless of credit if the applicant had sufficient income to make the monthly lease payment. He agreed to the terms but a down payment was needed to secure the deal. I would love to tell you that we found $850 behind a rock but I would be lying. Once again, I took a learning experience away from him and provided a fix instead. I am embarrassed and even ashamed at my failure to make Josh be accountable and stand on his own two feet. It is the quality in my life that I am least proud of and even though I have a loud bark, I have become very passive to a fault.

Josh had burned bridges at almost every doctor's office and emergency room back home from trying to get pills for his addiction. Once he had even went as far as getting teeth pulled unnecessarily in order to be prescribed pain medication. While at our home, he had a bad episode of anxiety and went to a local veteran's hospital for help. He wasn't fooling anyone and a call from Millie resulted in him being forced to stay there for a week. All it did was make him angry and he felt like he needed to be out of his parent's home and on his own. His social worker agreed because he had more than sufficient income to support himself. We found a nearby apartment but he needed a deposit and first month's rent in order to secure it. I won't tell you who paid it. Just as soon as he moved in with what little stuff he had and with what Matt gave him, he decided to bring the girl down from West Virginia to live with him so he could continue in his role as self proclaimed savior. It lasted four days before he took her home having realized they were both a mess and he couldn't help her when he couldn't even help himself. Just two weeks into the first month of his apartment and he is sleeping on our couch. We go ahead and move him back home with us and hopefully now things will get better and they did for a few days.

He showed signs of being responsible by arranging to pay the over $1,200 in fines he received from his tickets in West Virginia but he just couldn't stay away from the girl. When he was thinking clearly, he would say over and over how he knew it couldn't work unless they both were clean from drug use. But when he was irrational, which was most of the time; he was consumed by her and the thought of them making a life together. After making a trip to see her one day, he was on his way home when something he had taken caused him to fall asleep and you guessed it, he had another wreck. He was almost in sight of home when the accident happened but this time, he was arrested for a DWI and taken to the regional jail. After all those years of accidents, driving under the influence and getting away with it, he now found himself in jail for the first time in his life. Of course, bail money had to be paid for him to be released and the car he had leased was damaged pretty badly and something underneath had busted and let the oil out.

After I paid the towing bill, it was taken to the dealership for repair and his insurance company provided a rental that was much nicer than the car he wrecked! Sometimes it seems like crime does pay! I wanted to scream when I saw the nice Chrysler he was driving. Instead of feeling accountable, here he was with a super nice car, his bail paid by ole dad and he's back home rent free again. Was it God blessing him with another chance or just the devil messing with him to keep him from changing his behavior? By now, I had no clue, I thought it was all my fault and it probably was because I still had not learned how to say no.

Swearing he had learned his lesson from the DWI, we had a couple weeks of fairly normal behavior until a deputy showed up at our door one afternoon. As I have already stated, after leaving my church I continued driving a school bus but had also began working part time at the local Walmart. I had just finished my evening bus route and was on my way to my second job when Matt called to tell me Josh had been arrested for missing his court date. This time Millie had to go to the jail to bail him out and she was not a happy camper. Believing it was a simple oversight, we moved forward and was actually considering relocating to another part of the state where I was a candidate for Pastor of a church in our conference. However, I couldn't escape the uneasiness in my spirit and I eventually withdrew from consideration. I was afraid that even though Josh said he wanted to go, that he would change his mind at the last minute or move up there and then decide to move back after we were settled. I felt like I couldn't take the chance that he might end up somewhere alone so I backed out of contention for Pastor and we stayed put.

The thought of jail time, which was a real possibility, plus the fact he was going to lose his driver's license at least for a short time, led Josh to decide to let the lease car go back to the dealer. He concluded there was no need to pay for a car he was unlikely to be able to drive so when the car was fixed he informed them of his decision and returned the rental car. His court date was still about seven weeks away and he wouldn't have any decision on his penalties until then but he still had a license and still needed transportation. I know you are probably screaming at this book for me not to do it but I did it anyway. I had a good friend who had a 2004 Lincoln with 200,000 miles on it and he sold it to me for seventeen hundred dollars. I titled it in Josh's name and figured at least the big car would offer more protection if he had an accident. It was just a few days when I noticed a big scratch on the driver side resulting from an encounter with something but I didn't know what.

I can't swear that what I am about to tell you is completely the truth, but it is as far as I can tell based on my own personal encounters and Josh's story. Josh said he received a call from the girl in West Virginia and she told him that she was pregnant and contemplating an abortion. I don't know exactly what was said but apparently, the baby belonged to someone she went to a party with and Josh lost it; I mean he completely lost all ability to think reasonably and intelligently. On a trip to West Virginia he received a second DWI but again was released, driver's license intact and actually was allowed to drive home. I don't understand it but he seemed to get penalized the least amount possible but things were adding up. He knew now that jail time was likely and he couldn't handle the thought of it. Then there was the girl and the baby which left him in such a state of anxiety he was about to explode. He actually chewed the insides of his mouth into a raw mass of tissue. He even took the title of the Lincoln to a loan company and borrowed money which he said he gave to the girl. Based on his behavior, it is just as likely it was for drugs but again, I don't know and it doesn't really matter now.

As I sit here and type these words, my stomach ties up in knots when I visualize the last weeks of Josh's life. He couldn't sleep, couldn't eat and found peace in nothing. I hate drug abuse, addiction, depression and bipolar disorder and never want to see anyone go through what he did. God wanted so much more for him and gifted him with skills and talents to make real contributions to society and especially, the Kingdom of God but the thief really had it out for him. He stole from him, destroyed him and eventually took his life all the while denying him the privilege of reaching his potential. Please don't let the same thing happen to someone you love.

Convinced the pregnancy was his fault and saving the child was his responsibility, Josh said he offered to marry the girl and raise the baby as his own. I am not sure if he actually told her that but he told us that he did many times. He believed an abortion would be his fault because he had taken her back home after she moved here with him. We tried and tried to convince him he was not responsible but he would not listen to reason. He was totally a wreck and tried for a few days to get some anxiety medication to calm himself down, but his medical records followed him around and no one would prescribe him anything including the veteran's hospital. He had hit bottom where his future included losing his driver's license and probable jail time. He had lost everything and for the first time in his life, he was facing consequences beyond his ability to manipulate the outcome. He was pitiful and aggravating at the same time. Every emotion filled our home and everyone walked on egg shells as not to provoke him but enough was enough.

On Monday, June 6, I searched the internet for a long term facility equipped to treat someone over an extended period of time in order to give them a better chance of recovery. I found one that was Christian based and only charged an application fee which I would have gladly paid, but there was the problem of methadone. Most facilities can't or won't treat a patient until they are off of methadone and before I could verify the requirements of this particular facility, an argument broke out. For the first time in my life, I stood up to Josh and told him to stop using methadone as a crutch. We exchanged unpleasant words and he even got physical while saying some very hurtful and ugly things to me. I had to physically hold him away and he was completely shocked to see me stand up to him. It all happened so fast but I wish that I had let his arms go and just gave him a hug. You know the kind you give until the emotion of the moment dissipates but I will never know if it would have mattered and I never got the chance to hug him again.

After the argument, I left for work and apparently, the situation continued to deteriorate with Millie and Matt. Eventually, Millie went to the emergency department because she was having a breakdown and Matt went downstairs. They thought if they gave Josh some space he would cool off but soon after, he left too. We never spoke again except for some unpleasant texts he sent me later that evening and the next time I saw him, he was on life support at Roanoke Memorial Hospital. I will go to my grave believing if I had only been more of a stumbling block and less of an enabler he might still be with us today. I can't and won't accept responsibility for his death because he made the wrong choices which led there, but I do feel that better decisions on my part could have made a difference.

I know God desired a better life for Josh; we just failed to find it. I knew in my spirit and I even told Millie that this latest episode was not going to end well. Was I being faithless? I don't think so because I have grown to know that all of God's maneuvering in and out of our lives is not readily visible to us and He doesn't need my permission or a specific prayer to work His wonders or His will all around us.

There are so many things I will never be able to say to my son that I needed to say and he needed to hear. I want him to know how proud I was of his accomplishments in the Air Force. I want him to know I bragged about his honor performances in school and college and how I admired his love for music and his desire to play drums for the Lord in church. I wish I could tell him he was a good provider for his family and it made me so happy to see his generosity. I want him to know how much I envied his artistic talent and how I thought he was specially gifted by God. There is so much more I wish I had said. Oh, I said these things to him throughout his life but I am talking about the last time I saw him. Instead of him hearing how much he meant to me, my son heard an argument as the last words his dad spoke to him. Please don't let the same thing happen to you. Believe me, winning or losing an argument means nothing when you never get the chance to clear things up with the one you argued with.

CHAPTER 13

Every Parent's Nightmare

Most adults can tell you in a split second the when, where and what of their lives the day terrorist's struck the Twin Towers and Pentagon on September 11, 2001. I was on my way to the very same hospital in Roanoke to pick up my dad who was being discharged after having a stint put in the area around his heart. That day was one of life's moments that made for a lasting impression on everyone. For as long as most of us live, we will remember that day and those events with vivid pictures in our minds of the towers crumbling to the ground. I can also tell you where I was the first time I heard the song "Blessings" by Christian Recording Artist and Author, Laura Story. That song touched something way down deep in my soul and I still love to hear it today. I was sitting in the parking lot of a Dollar General Store in Rich Creek, Virginia, waiting for one of Cornerstone's Council Members to meet me. We were going to the home of a former Cornerstone Pastor to visit with his widow the day following his untimely death. She was not at home at the time but I was able to meet her later at her husband's viewing.

He had been Cornerstone's Pastor during some of its most active and productive years and had led the congregation through a building program resulting in a beautiful new sanctuary seating 250 – 300 people. He was a visionary to say the least, and a great teacher of the scriptures as well as a gifted artist. He was a great Pastor and was held in high regard by the leaders of our Conference. By the way, I share his story with permission of his wife who hopes anyone reading this can be encouraged by his story. In addition to being a great minister and teacher, he was also a recovering drug addict and one who struggled with occasional relapses and deep depression. Just like Josh, he found himself living a life he knew was not designed for him in heaven, fighting a losing battle having succeeded at taking his own life while staying at a rehab facility. He had just returned from a church service and those with him said he was blessed by what he experienced and it seemed to help him but yet, the weight of guilt and the dungeon of depression was more than he could handle.

The details of his suicide are not important but the sadness of leaving a wife and three wonderful children are. I am sure they will always have unanswered questions just as we will but I pray they have the same peace which God has gently massaged into our hearts as the days pass since we lost Josh. I can't help but believe there is something, somehow to be done to bring help to those who struggle at such a level but I only know that so far, we have failed to find it.

On the Tuesday, between the Monday of our argument and the Wednesday of Josh's accident, I started reading a book written by the aforementioned author, Laura Story. The title of the book is; "When God Doesn't Fix It" and it is the story of her family and how they navigated through her husband's brain tumor, surgery and continuing recovery. I won't spoil it for you but would recommend it highly for anyone and especially for those who seem to be facing a never ending battle. I actually finished the book while Josh was in his coma and it was, and is a great source of inspiration and insight for me. It is far above my pay grade and many people would cringe at the thought of saying it, but, for whatever reason, sometimes God doesn't fix it. Doesn't mean He can't, doesn't mean the situation is His perfect will, doesn't mean we should quit praying, all I am saying is sometimes it doesn't get fixed. But, just because problems aren't always solved doesn't mean God has abandoned us, it only means we have an opportunity to learn His grace is sufficient.

We were visiting my mom when my cell phone rang at eleven a.m. that Wednesday morning. The person identified themselves as a patient representative for Carilion Roanoke Memorial Hospital and she proceeded to tell me a young man had been air lifted to their facility from an automobile crash site in Giles County, Virginia and they had been trying for two hours to locate a next of kin. Next of kin? No, he wasn't deceased but he was in critical condition and on life support. She asked me several questions trying to confirm if Josh was my son. One question was to see if I could identify four things in his wallet. I said no but one thing he would have for sure would be a veteran's identification card. She said he was my son and we should get to the hospital as soon as we could.

The two hour drive took three years but we finally got there. There were no major lacerations, no visible scrapes or bruises but there was a big lump on the back of his head and it was obvious why he was in a coma. I chose to not speak to the investigating officer of the crash because knowing details would not change the outcome and frankly, I didn't think I would find out anything I probably didn't already suspect or know. To this day, I still haven't seen the accident report nor have I seen the car he crashed in. Friends from Cornerstone were kind enough to gather what things remained and give them to Matt.

On our way to the hospital we contacted Matt and then let some of our extended family members know so they could spread the word and have people begin praying. We both called some of our friends at Cornerstone to let them know what had happened because so many of them were familiar with Josh's struggles. Just like wild fire on windy day, the news spread and people from all over began reaching out to us and praying. Josh was moved to the ICU and placed on multiple IV drips which provided him with pain medications, antibiotics, fluids and liquid nutrition. I had set with him for days on similar life support a few years earlier during his attempt at suicide but this time was different because these measures now were actually keeping him alive. The first time the coma was medically induced to allow his body to heal but now the coma was the result of his severe brain trauma.

The way the doctor's described his brain injury left us mystified but still amazed at God's creative design. It seems that the trauma to his brain had disconnected the signals usually sent out to the body which we identify as movement and reflex. The brain was sending signals but they were "misfiring" and sort of sputtering. That's the best way I know to explain it but one thing was sure, apart from a miracle, even if he regained consciousness Josh would never be the same. As we look back we can clearly see that all the medical professionals held little, if any, hope of him waking up. Each time they spoke to us the words "severe brain trauma" were used with emphasis many times describing the word "severe" with multiple "very's".

They were graciously giving us time to connect to the severity of the situation and never rushed us to any premature judgment or conclusion.

We had only been at the hospital a short time on that Wednesday before friends, family, co-workers and ministry associates began arriving to stand by us, pray and offer their love and support. I would love to mention every name but it would just sound like a roll call from the largest class at school and I am sure I would leave someone out. But I will mention my mom, Geneva, who was the only grandparent Josh had left and whom also had a close and special bond with him. On oxygen and in a wheel chair, she had made the two hour trip fearing this may be her last opportunity to ever see her oldest grandson. The flow of support continued throughout the ten day ordeal with visitor's constantly flowing in and out bringing food, gifts and offering prayers. Financial support came from all over as so many knew how costly it is to basically live at a hospital plus folks also knew I had to take a leave of absence from my job at Walmart. That is what I want people to understand about the grace of God when things don't get fixed like we want them to. God sees and knows what we do not and He never leaves us or withdraws His mercy from us.

Have you ever felt prayer? Let me explain what I mean; have you ever recognized a strength in the face of overwhelming circumstances that you knew you were living above your own capabilities? That is how we felt during our stay with Josh in the hospital. Although we knew his prognosis was bleak unless a miracle came, we sensed the Holy Spirit continually and knew God was right there with us. We did so, because hundreds, probably even thousands of people were offering prayers for us every day. I liken it unto an individual being lifted in the air and passed around on the fingertips of a crowd. We have seen it at sporting events and concerts so I think you can understand what I am saying. I sat in the waiting room for hours during the late evenings and nights and was able to minister to others who were engaged in their own struggle sharing our testimony and the love of Christ with them. Only God can enable a man or woman to do such ministry at such a time and He certainly helped me. My daily posts on FaceBook updating Josh's condition sparked support, concern and prayers from people we will never meet or get a chance to thank.

Such an experience will cause a person to realize we are not alone while facing the tragedies of life. Being a Pastor for fifteen consecutive years had actually separated me from the realities existing in the lives of others outside of the church. As a Pastor, I controlled my environment but now, working two jobs and seeing the world through secular eyes, I have come to see that the world is full of pain and I hope this experience makes me a better Minister when I return to a pulpit.

Day by day the team of doctor's came to examine Josh, answer questions and then move on to their next patient. They took all the time we required but each examination failed to show any signs of improvement. A pressure tube was inserted into Josh's skull which monitored brain swelling and each time a certain point was reached, a valve was opened to drain fluid. It wasn't blood; it was spinal fluid being released through the brain because of the pressure. It was not an easy thing to watch and we had no idea how much pain our son was in. After a few days, they began to talk to us about a tracheotomy, permanent feeding tube and long term nursing care. We had to consider the possibility Josh may never wake up and they had no way to predict any quality of life if he did. Of course, the longer he was in the coma, the least likely it would be that he would ever wake up and he had expressed many times he never wanted to be kept alive with machines. We were told extended ventilator use would lead to infection so we would be faced with a critical decision very soon if things didn't improve. Regrettably, there was no improvement.

My heart still breaks today as I remember the pain Josh lived with. Yes, his poor decision making and lifestyle behaviors were enough to make you want to scream, but his suffering and illness was real and it robbed him of any measure of peace in this life. He believed he was the biggest disappointment who ever lived. He had no self-confidence and his failures tormented him. The last few weeks of his life were miserable for him and the last thing he said to his mother was he wasn't worthy of prayer. Can you imagine being so depressed you think you are not worth praying for? Maybe we have for a brief moment but that was the mentality Josh lived with.

He told Millie he wished he had not been spared from his suicide attempt and had never awakened from the medically induced coma. He was facing the loss of his license, financial consequences from bad decisions and most likely jail time. He had said he just wished he could get some sleep and ironically, the doctor's told us the area of his brain which was injured was the area that would put someone into a deep sleep. Millie and

I actually saw the hand of God releasing mercy to Josh to give him some much needed rest. Even though a tragedy had occurred, God was working things together for Josh's well being. We need to understand that even though our lives may not always work out according to the perfect plan of God, He never abandons us and He stays with us until the end. Those are shouting words!

Millie and I were scheduled to minister at a church in Staunton, Virginia on the Sunday Josh was in the hospital and I felt like I should at least go and honor the commitment. The church was a little more than an hour away from the hospital and I felt like I could return very promptly if needed, but Millie chose to stay with Josh so I went alone. During the praise & worship a lady came to where I was standing and said this to me; "I don't know your son but God has impressed upon me to tell you not to worry about him because He is communing with him and spiritual healing is happening." Those may not be the exact words but it is the message she felt she needed to share with me. I just smiled and kept worshiping because God truly is worthy of all praise. No more than a day or two passed until someone else in another part of the state, sent us a message saying practically verbatim, the same thing. We were saddened at the condition of our son while at the same time rejoicing over the faithfulness and compassion of our God!

Just a few weeks before the accident, Josh had attended services with us at a church not far from where we lived as I filled in for a friend who was out of town. From the moment I began my message until the end, Josh sat and cried as the Lord was doing a work in his heart. For several days the impact from the intimacy with the Lord stayed with him as he talked about changes he needed to make and things he needed to start doing again. It was very refreshing and encouraging for us but little did we realize at the time, that God had begun a work that day and now He was completing it as our son lay in a coma. I think the worst thing organized religion has done to hurt simple Christianity is so many of us at times feel like we have to have an exact knowledge of God. We feel like we have to explain His ways even though He tells us they are far higher than our own ways. I say we let God be God and if something needs explained let's leave it up to Him. Isn't that really the essence of what faith truly is?

CHAPTER 14

We Say Goodbye

After seven full days of life support, deep coma and no signs of improvement in brain function and reflex action, we knew a tough decision was ahead but we still were not ready to make it. During that Tuesday night, Josh's body began jerking at times and he also began to raise his legs. Millie was asleep in the chair beside his bed and I was resting in the waiting area. She awakened to find two nurses and a doctor standing by the bed sort of just staring at what was going on. They began to explain that the movement was most likely caused by what they described as "neuro-storms" in Josh's brain and could very well indicate he might be feeling severe pain. It seems like his brain was "firing" but missing every mark and this resulted in the random movements.

We met with the team of physicians, asked every possible question we could think of and since there had been no improvement, we told them we couldn't bear the thought of him suffering so Millie and I agreed to remove him from the ventilator. Although the decision was ours alone to make, we had the consensus of agreement from the rest of our family including Matt and Melissa. If he could continue to breathe on his own then we were prepared to consider long term care options but if not, we were equally prepared to release him into the arms of Jesus. At least as prepared as parents can be.

We called family and close friends and informed them of our decision to remove him from the ventilator which was scheduled for later that afternoon. As had been the case all along, we were surrounded by love and support as they continued to arrive at the hospital during the day. No one knew what would happen but they were not going to let us go through it alone. The doctor took the family back to a room to answer any questions and to tell us what the procedures would be. Everyone was crying as we headed back to Josh's room to say our goodbye's to him. Millie, Matt, Melissa, my mom and I went in first. I think others may have been in the room at the time but I can't be sure. One by one we told him we loved him and we would see him again in heaven. After we finished, we invited family and friends into the room to do the same. I wish he could have realized how much he was loved here in this life and I have prayed and asked God to tell him.

There are a lot of goodbye's we say to our children. The first time we leave them with someone after they are born so mom and dad can have a few hours alone. Perhaps it's the first day of school, when they leave our care for a few hours and are entrusted to someone else to watch over them. Then there is the first time they spend the night with a friend and are away from us as today becomes tomorrow. And also, there is the first time they drive a car alone and are out of our sight and control for an entire evening. Or maybe like all the times we waved our goodbyes as Josh, and then Melissa, parted our company heading back to North Dakota. All of those types of goodbye have something in common and that is the anticipation of seeing them again when they get home or make a return trip. However, none of them prepare you to say the kind of goodbye you say when you are letting your loved one slip away from this life into eternity. I know we will meet again but to think there will never be another hug, handshake or smile here in this life is just not the same goodbye.

The doctor removed the ventilator and the oddest thing happened, Josh yawned. Just like you and I do after a nap or night's sleep, he yawned. It was like Millie had said all along, God had given him the sleep he needed so desperately. However, he didn't wake up, didn't open his eyes or stretch like we do when we awaken, he just yawned. But he did keep breathing on his own. His respiration was very fast and his heart was beating 160 times per minute, but he was still here and managing on his own. Sadly, it wasn't long until signs began appearing showing us he was having difficulty making it without the artificial means of support.

He spent Wednesday night in the ICU but on Thursday morning, the decision was made to move him to the Palliative Care Unit on the same floor. During the day on Thursday we continued to have visitor's who provided tremendous love and support for us but Josh's condition continued to decline. Melissa and Matt played some of his favorite music and we talked with him telling him how much we loved him. We entered the evening hours with the nurses managing his pain and watched as his fever climbed to 105 degrees and his breaths becoming more and more difficult. At 4:50 a.m. on Friday morning, Josh left this life and slipped into the arms of Jesus with his mom and dad by his bedside as the last breath was taken. It wasn't dramatic, he just exhaled and did not inhale again.

I wavered for just a moment as to if we should bury him in a country cemetery where some of our family was buried or in the Southwest Virginia Veteran's Cemetery which is actually located across the road from where we lived at the time in Dublin, Virginia. Melissa also has quite a few members of her family buried in the country cemetery and it seemed like a good thing to bury him near people he knew. However, Matt was adamant that Josh be placed in the Veteran's Cemetery because he had told him several times that is where he wanted to be if something ever happened to him. I took what Matt said to heart and went immediately to finalize the arrangements to have Josh placed there. It was the best choice because Josh's accomplishments in the Air Force were the greatest in his life so it made perfect sense he be buried in a cemetery where he would be remembered and appreciated for his service to our country.

We anticipated a large crowd for the viewing and funeral service and I feared the funeral home chapel might not accommodate the people. I asked the new Pastor at Cornerstone if we could use the church and have the Praise Team sing a few songs and of course, he was more than generous in saying yes so everything was set. To honor Josh's wishes, only the family was allowed to view his body before the public was allowed in the sanctuary and the remainder of the evening was spent with a closed coffin and an American Flag covering it. A steady flow of family and friends made their way up front to speak with us and share their love and condolences all the way up to service time.

There were a large number of minister friends with their spouses, friends from the community where we had been a Pastor for all those years, friends from work, those Josh and Melissa both went to school with, friends of Matt's, many from Melissa's family, former church members from Austinville and of course, most everyone from Cornerstone Church. It was overwhelming to say the least.

Little Amy from kindergarten who gave Josh a kiss so he would be her friend was there. Minister's who had participated in Bible Quiz competitions when Josh was younger were there. Friends and the Pastor from the church he and Melissa attended were there. Those from past churches who coached him and watched him grow up were there. The list could go on and on. When the evening was over a count of nearly 500 visitors was made. The church which seats 250 – 300 was filled with some standing in the back during the memorial service. We will always be grateful for the outpouring of support shown to us during the entire ordeal and we hope to be as kind to others in their time of need. Matt set up a four table display of Josh's military awards and some of his art work and people were amazed at how gifted and talented he was. People literally lingered from table to table as they learned about a side of Josh they were never aware of.

If there ever was a good funeral, his was. The Praise Team sang "Amazing Grace My Chains are Gone," Matt read a speech he had prepared, I conducted the service and Millie led several family members in singing; "Go Rest High." We buried him the next morning with full military honors as Air Force Airmen folded the flag while the local VFW gave the gun salute. It was the best, and the least we could do as we said our final goodbye's. And just like that, at age thirty nine, we had to let our son go and now we are left with looking back to see what we may have done differently which could have contributed to a more positive outcome in his life. And just like before, two completely different individuals from two different geographical areas, sent us word that God had shown them that Josh would not come back if he could. Thank you Lord for Your goodness!

CONCLUSION

Ever since Adam and Eve disobeyed God in the Garden of Eden, the consequences of their sin have been wreaking havoc on all of mankind. Just like a stone tossed into a placid lake, the ripple of sin continues to spread its destructive influence among every succeeding generation. It's not just evident in the lives of those battling addiction or suffering from depression, but we see it in every aspect of history and modern society. It shows up in hatred, prejudices and disrespect for God and others every day. We see it in senseless killings on our streets and abortion of the unborn as well as persecution, oppression and genuine unfairness and lack of concern in all nations. Sin has given birth to a global society of self centered people in which love has truly grown cold. Whether we want to admit or not, our lives and the lives of those we love, have in some measure suffered from the consequences of sin in this world.

However, all is not lost and hope endures for every man, woman, girl and boy on planet earth. The hope I refer to is not a rabbit's foot or four leaf clover, it is a person. Hope is offered to all today because Jesus Christ came and died to pay the penalty for sin in this world. He then rose from the dead breaking the authority of sin in the lives of those who would place faith in Him. He is a greater stone cast into that placid lake and the ripple effect of having Christ in your life is far greater than the effect of sin. Even though we still battle the remnants of sin in our flesh, Jesus has equipped us to be over-comers in this world and has sealed us with His Spirit as the down payment for our redemption. Although not complete until Christ returns, the power of His redemption has set us free from the darkness and authorities of sin in this world and one day, redemption will be consummated and all the consequences and effects of sin won't even be a memory. Glory to God!

Josh struggled with addiction and depression for more than a decade and some might say he lost the battle. I say he just fought until the end. There are more still in the battle and perhaps it is someone you know and love or, it may even be you. My hope is that you will fight, not give in and fight some more. If someone you love is trapped in addiction don't give up on them. Don't be afraid to confront them early on and you may avoid the mistakes I made. Don't be an enabler and learn not to believe their lies no matter how desperate and heart breaking they may be. Learn to say no and mean it. Keep praying and trusting God and if it doesn't get fixed like you think it should be, just know He is somehow working it together for good. Just don't deny the problem and bury your head in the sand because apart from divine intervention, it will not go away.

Don't be afraid to share your story, you will be amazed at how many people will open up to you and let you know they are facing the same or a similar struggle. I met an elderly grandmother in Walmart who was still mourning the tragic loss of her twenty one year old grandson. We shared our stories and each of us shed some tears as we hugged one another right there in front of everyone. The world is filled with hurting people and knowing you hurt too might be the edge they need to seek help. I am not opposed to any kind of treatment that has a focus on helping people but never forget that God alone is the healer. Even though you might be filled with questions always include God in whatever steps you choose to take. He will never let you down. We now wait for the glorious day of resurrection when we will see our son again and so I conclude with my favorite five words of scripture penned by the Apostle John; "Even so, come, Lord Jesus." (Revelation 22:20 KJV)

ABOUT THE AUTHOR

John B. Jenkins, a native of Southern West Virginia, has a background as a coal miner, nonprofit executive, and pastoral minister. He holds an associate's degree in Christian education from Maranatha College of Christian Ministries, Dublin, Virginia. He and Millie, his high school sweetheart and wife, celebrated their fortieth anniversary in March 2016.